'Another fabulous resource from 10of1... people to dig into the Bible and get to know Jesus, their King. Chris Ranson has used wonderful illustrations, dry humour and simple language to help teenagers engage with life-changing theology that is applied to their lives.'

NICK JACKMAN,
DIRECTOR OF CONTAGIOUS

'In an increasingly biblically illiterate and post-truth age, our young people are searching for meaning and hungry for authenticity. Relevant, creative and faithful ways of unpacking the story of Jesus are desperately needed. Dig Into Matthew is beautifully crafted, rich in deep biblical explanation and I am delighted to commend it to you. Chris Ranson unpacks the gospel with humour, ingenuity and passion. This book is a gift to a generation.'

PHIL KNOX,
HEAD OF MISSION TO YOUNG ADULTS, EVANGELICAL ALLIANCE

'Dig Into Matthew will help teens do what it says on the tin – delve into the depths of Matthew's gospel and get to God's promised King. Its chatty humour makes it accessible, the accompanying illustrations bring clarity and simplicity, and the questions encourage engagement and action. Altogether, a great resource!'

TAMAR POLLARD,
GRACE COMMUNITY CHURCH, BEDFORD

British Library Cataloguing in Publication Data
A record for this book is available from the British Library

ISBN: 978-1-913278-35-9

Designed and typeset by Pete Barnsley (CreativeHoot.com)
Illustrations by Chris Ranson

Printed in China

10Publishing, a division of 10ofthose.com
Unit C, Tomlinson Road, Leyland, PR25 2DY, England

Email: info@10ofthose.com
Website: www.10ofthose.com

1 3 5 7 10 8 6 4 2

DIG INTO
MATTHEW

A DAILY BIBLE STUDY

CHRIS RANSON

10 Publishing
a division of 10ofthose.com

To my parents

INTRODUCTION

God's people had been waiting. They had been waiting a really long time. In fact, imagine being stuck in a traffic jam, your phone has run out of battery and now you need to make a rest stop – that's the kind of waiting the Israelites were doing. But why? What were they waiting for? Well, that's the wrong question ... the real question is who were they waiting for?

Thousands of years before, God had promised His people a King; a special King who would start a new, special Kingdom. This King would be so powerful that His Kingdom would last forever and nobody would be able to defeat Him. One day, around 2000 years ago, that King finally arrived. Thankfully, when this happened Matthew was around to write down what happened – and it's not what you might think!

There's a long journey ahead as we dig into Matthew together. You may have lots of questions like: 'What did this King do?' 'Why did God come to earth as a human?' And 'why on earth is John the Baptist eating locusts?'

Not only will you be getting your hands dirty with some of the nitty gritty bits of the Bible, but you will also get to know this promised King for yourself – and trust me, you won't want to miss out on that!

God speaks to us through His word and the book of Matthew is no different. It is my prayer that as you take time each day to read the passage and use this book that God's word will seem more true to you than ever before, and His King more precious.

A JOURNEY BEGINS

Wow! Did you really just pray that? 'Your Kingdom come?' That is a huge thing to just mumble along with in church! Have you ever thought what it really means?

THERE IS A KINGDOM

Seems obvious now you read it, but it can be easy to miss: God has a Kingdom! It's not a physical place like the United Kingdom or the Kingdom of Tonga … you can't catch a flight there. Instead, this Kingdom is made up of every person who lives like God wants them to.

But a Christian doesn't get a passport to prove they are in God's Kingdom. So how can you tell if you're in or not? It comes down to one simple fact: how do you respond to the King?

THERE IS A KING

Whoops! Nearly forgot! God's Kingdom has a King! If you pray for God's Kingdom to come, you're not only praying that you want things on earth to be like God wants them to be (peaceful, fair, loving, giving glory to Him) but you are also praying that God's King will come!

This King came once before and He turned the whole world upside down. Matthew wrote what happened in his history book, but that is not the end of the story. If you keep reading, you will see that God's King is right now sitting on a throne in heaven and He has promised to come again. This means that *in the future*, the Kingdom will come. When that happens all evil and rebellion against the King will be defeated. But right now, amazingly, it means that anyone in God's Kingdom has a powerful King working for their best – the King of the universe is on their side, today!

DOESN'T THAT CHANGE THINGS?

God's King, the most powerful King in the world, wants the best for you. (Yes you, reading this book!) There are always other books you can read, other things you could be doing, friends you could be seeing – but why not set aside a little time each day so we can read Matthew's incredible true story? The King of Kings is calling you: do you want to hear what He has to say?

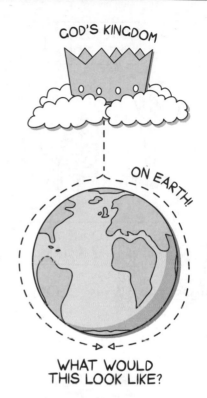

GOD'S KINGDOM

ON EARTH!

WHAT WOULD THIS LOOK LIKE?

QUESTIONS

- If you could meet the King of the universe - what questions would you ask Him? Write them down and pray to God about them.

- As we go through Matthew, make a note of any answers you get.

MORE THAN A LIST (1:1-17)

Think lists are boring? Think again! Matthew starts his action-packed true story about Jesus with a long list of names called a 'genealogy'. Matthew isn't a nerd – he is using this list to tell us that Jesus descended from mighty kings (like David) and also from everyday normal people (like Ruth).

For the Jews, who Matthew was writing to, this was really important. You see, God had made big promises to care for His chosen people throughout history. Starting with Abraham (name number one!) these promises were to be passed down through generations of God's people until they would one day reach the 'Messiah', the one chosen person to make all these promises come true – He is kind of a big deal.

WHAT'S IN A NAME? (1:1)

In his first line, Matthew manages to squeeze in *four* different names for Jesus, each with their own meaning. Is he just showing off? Nope! Each of

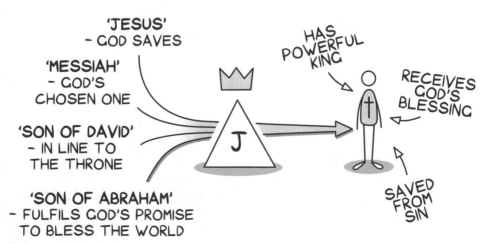

these titles tells us something very important about Jesus.

As we find out in Matthew 1:21, 'Jesus' means 'the Lord saves'. So when someone says 'Jesus', we are reminded that God saves His people through something that Jesus did (John 3:16, Romans 6:23).

'Messiah' is the same name as 'Christ'. These titles mean 'Chosen One'. When God made promises to His people, He also chose one individual to make the promises happen.

'Son of David' reminds us that Jesus is a direct descendent of King David, the greatest King in Jewish history. Things went well when David was in charge, but things will be perfect when King Jesus is on the throne.

'Son of Abraham' takes us back to the promise (or the covenant) that God made to bless all the people of the earth through Abraham. The amazing promises God made to Abraham will only ever come about through Jesus (You can see these promises in Genesis 12:1–3; 17:3–7.)

THE UNASHAMED KING

If you research this list of names, you will notice that many of them are utter rascals! Jacob was a scam artist, the brothers of Judah were bullies, Rahab was a prostitute and even David was a murderer; yet God used all these people to bring about the arrival of Jesus. King Jesus is not ashamed to welcome broken or bad people into His Kingdom. Quite the opposite! This genealogy tells us that God's promises of love and care are open to *anyone* who comes to Him through the King.

QUESTIONS

- The Old Testament promises that God made to love and care become real in Jesus. How can you get to experience these promises?

- Look again at the four titles of Jesus. Pick one and thank God for what it means to you.

GOD WITH US!

A VIRGIN GIVES BIRTH? (1:18-21)

Quite the shocker! Mary became pregnant, even though she had never been romantically involved with a man. This miracle has never happened before in human history and will never happen again. Matthew tells us this child did not come about in any normal way – this was a miracle by the Holy Spirit.

The Holy Spirit was active at the creation of the world (Gen. 1:2), the Holy Spirit was active at Jesus' birth (Mat. 1:18), and today when we become a Christian, it is the Holy Spirit who makes us new people; He brings us into God's Kingdom and gives us the power to live the way God wants us to live. In other words, it is the same Holy Spirit who works a miracle at Jesus' birth who makes Christians 'born again' (John 3:3).

PROPHECY FULFILLED (1:22-25)

Isn't it amazing that these specific events were predicted nearly 700 years beforehand? It's hard enough to predict the weather where I live in Scotland (and the only options are rain or drizzle) never mind the birth of God's chosen King. But Matthew makes sure we realise this was all planned out

when in verse 22 he uses his trademark saying: 'All this took place to fulfil ...' God had planned from the beginning of time that one day He would live closely with His people. Our sin stops this from happening, but God had a plan to make the impossible possible – He would send this 'Immanuel' Jesus.

SPOT THE BIGGER PROBLEM!

SIN

ROMANS

HELP!

As the angel told Joseph in verse 21, Jesus will save His people from their biggest enemy. The Jews thought their enemy was the powerful Romans; many wanted Jesus to be a mighty warrior King who would kick the Roman army

JOSEPH, YOU'RE GOING TO BE THE MESSIAH'S ADOPTDED DAD... NO PRESSURE.

I PROMISE TO...

SIGNED: THE LORD

'COVENANT': A PROMISE THAT GOD MAKES WITH PEOPLE SO THAT WE MAY KNOW HIM. IN THE OLD COVENANT PEOPLE NEEDED SACRIFICES AND TEMPLE WORSHIP TO APPROACH GOD. HOWEVER, THIS ALL POINTED TO JESUS.

JESUS ESTABLISHED **THE NEW COVENANT** WHERE HIS SACRIFICE ON THE CROSS IS THE ONLY SACRIFICE WE NEED. HIS PEOPLE (CHRISTIANS) ARE THE TEMPLE WHERE GOD DWELLS AND WHERE WE CAN WORSHIP.

EPHESIANS 2:21-22

out of the country. But Jesus came to save us from a much bigger enemy: the sin that separates us from God.

AN ADOPTED CHILD (1:25)

If you have a keen eye, you may have noticed that Matthew's genealogy in 1:1–17 tells us Joseph was directly descended from King David. This means Joseph's son would inherit the right to become King of God's people. But Jesus was only the *biological* son of Mary, not Joseph, so how can He rightfully become King? He had to be adopted! What Matthew carefully records in 1:25 is that Joseph formally gave Jesus his name, and in the ancient world this legally meant the child was now Joseph's. (Thankfully, when your mates at school give you a nickname today, they haven't adopted you.)

QUESTIONS

If you're a Christian, God is with you at all times.

○ How will knowing this help you when you face hard times?

○ If you are a Christian and you sin, how do you think it affects the Holy Spirit who is within you?

LOCATION, LOCATION, LOCATION

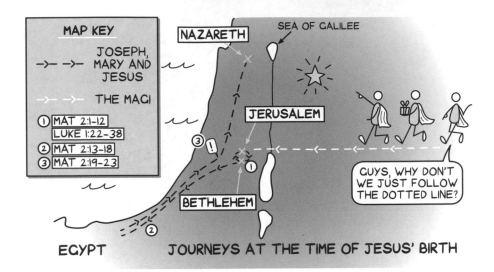

JOURNEYS AT THE TIME OF JESUS' BIRTH

WHERE IS JESUS FROM? (2:1-23)

If you have moved around a lot growing up, it can sometimes be hard to explain where you are from. Matthew had a trickier problem to explain in this section; where was *Jesus* from? Not only is He God (so He is not really 'from' anywhere – He has always existed) but the Old Testament prophecies spoke of the Messiah originating from three different locations on earth:

1. He was to come from Bethlehem. This was the birthplace of King David, and the new King would come from here too (v. 6).

2. God's Son (another title for Jesus), was to come out of Egypt like the Israelites first came out of Egypt in the book of Exodus (v. 15).

3. He was also to be a 'nobody'. People would think He was from nowhere important, and Nazareth was well known as a nowhere kind of place (v. 23).

The map above makes it look as if Jesus' parents had got lost on holiday, but really they were being chased around by killer men! But is that all that's happening? As you read Matthew 2:1–23, you can see that God was using these scary events to carefully guide Jesus and His family around in order that all the prophecies about Jesus would be fulfilled. Jesus

MOSES		JESUS
	THREATENED FROM BIRTH ☑	THREATENED FROM BIRTH
	SAVES GOD'S PEOPLE PHYSICAL SLAVERY ☑	SAVES US FROM SLAVERY TO SIN
	SPEAKS TO GOD ON BEHALF OF THE JEWS ☑	SPEAKS TO GOD ON OUR BEHALF
	LEADS GOD'S PEOPLE TO PROMISED LAND ☑	LEADS US TO ETERNAL PROMISED LAND

was from the birthplace of Kings, He was the Son of God called from Egypt and, despite all this, people rejected Him as a nobody from Nazareth.

THE NEW MOSES

If you read Exodus in the Old Testament (don't do it right now, it's a long book), you will see what Matthew saw; Jesus is a bigger and better Moses. Moses was one of the most important people to the Jews. With God's help, Moses rescued the Jews from slavery in Egypt and guided them into a land God promised to them. In a much bigger way, Jesus came to rescue us from slavery – slavery to sin! He makes it possible for us to follow Him instead of following our wrong desires. When we do this, Jesus guides us to

a place promised to us, a place of total peace and happiness. (You can read about this in Psalm 23.)

Despite the terrible evil that surrounded Jesus from the moment of His birth (1:16–18), God is still in control. When we feel that the dark things in life are getting the better of us, today we can remember that no matter what happens, God uses even the worst situations for our eventual good and His glory.

QUESTIONS

Jesus rules right now as King in heaven, but on earth He was rejected as a 'nobody'.

- Whose opinion was more important to Jesus: God's or other people's?

- Whose opinion is more important to you?

THE KING'S FIRST MOVES

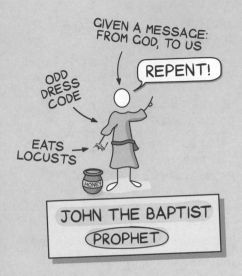

GIVEN A MESSAGE: FROM GOD, TO US

REPENT!

ODD DRESS CODE

EATS LOCUSTS

HONEY

JOHN THE BAPTIST
PROPHET

ONCE ATE A FLY FOR A DARE

GIVEN A MESSAGE: FROM HIS TEACHER ...TO HIS MUM

ODD DRESS CODE

YOUR MATE, STEVE
NOT A PROPHET

ENTRANCE INTO THE KINGDOM (3:1–6)

Read John's lips – 'no turning back!' When God's people crossed the Red Sea in Exodus, they escaped Egyptian slavery forever. When God's people crossed the River Jordan in Joshua, they escaped 40 years of desert wandering. Now, thousands of years later, John the Baptist stood in the same River Jordan calling for God's people to leave behind their lives of sin and prepare to enter the Kingdom of Heaven. 'The King is coming, get ready to follow Him!'

How did God's people do this? First, they would confess their sins; they would say how they were living in ways disobedient to God's laws. Second, they would be baptised to mark a point of change called repentance. This meant they had turned away from a sinful life, in order to live the way God wants.

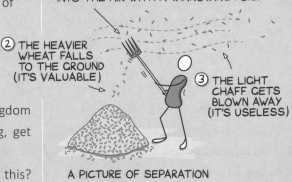

① HARVESTER THROWS WHEAT AND CHAFF INTO THE AIR WITH A WINNOWING FORK

② THE HEAVIER WHEAT FALLS TO THE GROUND (IT'S VALUABLE)

③ THE LIGHT CHAFF GETS BLOWN AWAY (IT'S USELESS)

A PICTURE OF SEPARATION

MAT. 3:12

This is a big deal, but John explains in verse 11 that his baptism points towards a more important one that Jesus would bring: a baptism with the Holy Spirit. Jesus' baptism could do more than John's. Jesus' baptism would make followers of God totally clean from sin and able to live in His coming Kingdom.

A WARNING (3:7-12)

The Jewish religious leaders at the time thought John was nuts — not because of the locust munching, but because of what he said! They thought being a biological descendant of Abraham automatically made them part of God's Kingdom, but John said they needed to repent. Outrageous! Or is it?

John gives a serious warning to this kind of thinking. Going to church does not make you a part of God's Kingdom. Jesus came to deal with our sin so that we can live with God. Therefore, only those who repent and have their sin forgiven by Jesus are part of His Kingdom. These Jewish leaders were in trouble!

THE BAPTISM OF JESUS (3:13-17)

Even though Jesus had never done anything wrong to repent of, our King chose to identify with His people by

VOICE OF THE FATHER

THIS IS MY SON

PICTURE OF THE SPIRIT (NOT ACTUALLY A DOVE!)

THE SON

J

being baptised. We are to look at Jesus and see a perfect example of how to live. If our King lives like God wants, then we should too.

After His baptism, Jesus comes up from the water and we get a quick 'behind the scenes' look at something amazing, an incredible moment. This newly arrived King is actually part of the Holy Trinity of God — King Jesus is God!

QUESTIONS

Repentance should be a part of our daily lives. Do you need to turn away from something that does not belong in God's Kingdom? Pray about this today and ask that God will help you to leave this sin behind.

IF YOU ARE THE SON OF GOD ...

JESUS DEFEATS THE DEVIL (4:1-11)

If Jesus is going to 'fulfil all righteousness' (Mat. 3:15) on behalf of His people, He must pass the tests that mankind always fail. He must resist temptation.

Adam and Eve in the garden of Eden? They failed to resist temptation (Gen. 3:1-6). God's people hungry in the desert? They failed to resist temptation (Ex. 16:1-3). Even today, Satan will try to tempt you with all sorts of things to pull you away from God – Christians can fail to resist temptation too.

But Jesus is different. He is better than Adam, the only perfect person out of all of God's people. He is never defeated by temptation and passes every test. The devil tempted Him with instant food, instant popularity and instant victory, but Jesus remained perfectly obedient to God's law (that's why He quotes it three times!). Finally, with the authority of a King, Jesus commands Satan to leave – and he does! Not even the devil himself can cause our King to fail!

If we try to fight the attacks of Satan with our own strength, we will *always*

4:18-22

ANDREW, I'M NOT SURE THIS IS WHAT JESUS MEANT BY 'FISHING FOR PEOPLE'

fail. (It would be like using a water pistol to fight a dragon ... even a wet dragon is going to chomp you down like you're one of John the Baptist's honey-coated locusts. Only Jesus has the power to defeat the devil – so stick close to Jesus in prayer. Only God's word (the Bible) is a useful weapon in this fight – so know your Bible like Jesus knew His. Some people think Bible reading and prayer are boring; what a mistake. It's hand-to-hand combat alongside our King, fighting for victory over evil! (Check out Ephesians 6:10–18.)

WHEN THE KING RULES ... (4:12-25)

... it is good news (v. 23)! Like many people today, you may get sad from looking at news broadcasts or from

ISRAEL'S 40 YEARS
CONSTANT COMPLAINING

DEUT 1:26-27;
9:7; 31:27...

JESUS' 40 DAYS
FAITHFUL FASTING

experiencing hard things in life. But, when Jesus picks up the message of John the Baptist in verse 17, it is good news for people like you. Jesus starts His Kingdom movement as it will continue: evil is defeated, the sick are healed and people are called to follow Him. Right now you may live in a world of darkness and pain. But for anyone who follows Jesus, this will only last for a short time. For those in His Kingdom, any suffering now will one day be banished forever by the King.

THE SON OF GOD...

...IS SUPERIOR TO ANGELS...
HEB 1:3

...RULES IN HEAVEN...
HEB 1:3

...CREATED & SUSTAINS THE UNIVERSE...
HEB 1:2-3

...SHINES WITH GOD'S GLORY...
HEB 1:3

...SPEAKS AS GOD...
HEB 1:2

...IS GOD AS A MAN...

QUESTIONS

- The next time you feel tempted to disobey God, what Bible verses will you use as a weapon to fight back?

- Why is it important for Christians to have a perfect, powerful King?

19

LIVING IN THE KINGDOM

The crowds from 4:25 have swamped Jesus looking for healing miracles. So many needy people! But in chapters 5 – 7, Jesus doesn't set up a hospital or a health clinic – He teaches about how to live in the Kingdom. Why? Because healed people will live for some time, but those in the Kingdom will live with God forever.

THE KINGDOM IS UPSIDE-DOWN (5:1–12)

The first thing that Jesus makes clear about God's Kingdom is that, for those who are in it, the world has been turned upside-down. (Unless you live in Australia, in which case you are already upside-down.)

The world tells us the most important people today are famous footballers, powerful politicians or amazing actresses. But Jesus' Kingdom doesn't value money, fame or power; Jesus' Kingdom is full of people who get beaten up by the world around them.

People who are humble before God and live like He commands, whatever the cost, they have been given the Kingdom of Heaven. People who mourn (are sad because of loss) will be comforted. Mighty warriors are not impressive to God, but those who make peace are called His children. Want to be a tough guy at school or the most popular person in the world? These things are worthless compared to what the King offers you.

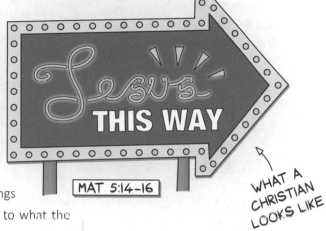

MAT 5:14-16

WHAT A CHRISTIAN LOOKS LIKE

So how can we show others what the King is like? Jesus gives us two helpful pictures.

BEING SALTY (5:13)

Have you ever accidently poured too much salt on your chips? Gross, right? Well, that's how others might feel about you being a salty Christian. Being salty means being different *from* the world in a way that helps keep the goodness of God *in* the world. Salty Christians preserve God's goodness on the planet – what a wonderful thing! But if we don't live like Jesus is our King, we become as useful as 'unsalty' salt and will be thrown away like a pile of old rocks.

BEING SHINY (5:14-16)

Forget bulbs and LEDs, God wants *us* to be lights in a dark world. Christians shine when they live a life of love and obedience that shows they are part of God's Kingdom. These lights direct the way to Jesus, and if we put them under a basket (or leave them behind at church on a Sunday) then nobody will ever see our King.

QUESTIONS

- Why would someone want to know the King and live as part of God's Kingdom (vv. 1-11)?

- Do people at school know you are a Christian? If not, perhaps it is time to be more salty and shiny!

21

THE LAW OF THE KING

HOWEVER JONATHAN TRIED TO MEASURE IT, THE RESULT WAS STILL THE SAME...

'RIGHTEOUS-OMETER'

SINNER — PERFECT LIKE GOD

NEEDS JESUS

JESUS AND OLD TESTAMENT LAW (5:17-20)

Have you ever wondered why God's Old Testament people (the Israelites) sacrificed animals but God's New Testament people (Christians) don't? It isn't because we've kicked the old rulebook into the church recycling. It's because Jesus Christ has fulfilled the Old Testament law (v. 17).

God's people had followed the same Old Testament law for centuries, and now it looked like Jesus was creating a new, easier law! But He wasn't. As Jesus makes clear, not only will the Old Testament law last until the end of time, but even people who think they have kept that law are kidding themselves! Yikes!

WHAT 'BEING GOOD' REALLY MEANS (5:21-48)

People might think you are a good person (or not!) but to be truly 'good' in God's eyes means not only doing right things on the outside, but thinking good things on the inside. For example, we all know that murder is wrong, but Jesus tells us that killing someone and hating someone comes from the same sinful place in your heart. If we ever hate somebody with our thoughts, God will judge us in a similar way to the person who hurts someone with their hands.

Being good is not about being nice or obeying a set of laws; it needs an *inward* change. In Jesus' time, people thought the Pharisees were obedient because they looked good on the outside, but people in Jesus' Kingdom

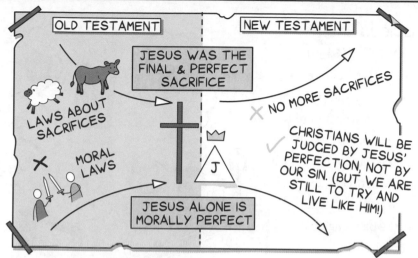

OLD TESTAMENT / NEW TESTAMENT

JESUS WAS THE FINAL & PERFECT SACRIFICE

LAWS ABOUT SACRIFICES

MORAL LAWS

JESUS ALONE IS MORALLY PERFECT

J

✗ NO MORE SACRIFICES

✓ CHRISTIANS WILL BE JUDGED BY JESUS' PERFECTION, NOT BY OUR SIN. (BUT WE ARE STILL TO TRY AND LIVE LIKE HIM!)

must be better, we need good thoughts as well as actions (v. 20)!

Amazingly, God makes this impossible task possible – the Holy Spirit works inside every Christian to transform their heart and mind. Incredible! Only after our inside has been changed will we see big change on the outside. Look how it affects our behaviour towards: friends, family and loved ones (vv. 21–32); the truth (vv. 33–37); people who hurt you (vv. 38–48).

BEING PERFECT (5:48)

Verse 48 is a big poke in the eye to anyone who thinks that God accepts them because they are a good person. Jesus says we must be more than good; we must be perfect. We can try our best to be

like Jesus, but everyone is a work in progress – nobody is perfect like the Father is perfect!

What a mystery! If nobody is perfect, how can anybody be part of God's perfect Kingdom? (We will come back to this head-scratcher later!) For now, the King has given us a clear picture of how His people are to live in His Kingdom – are you using His words as a guide?

QUESTIONS

- You may not have enemies (vv. 43-44), but how you treat outsiders to your group of friends matters.

- Why does Jesus want you to care about outsiders (vv. 45-48)?

OUR FATHER IN HEAVEN

RELIGIOUS LIKE A HYPOCRITE (6:1-6)

What's the difference between good religion and bad religion? It all depends on why we are religious; do we want to be thought well of by *people* or do we care about what *God* thinks? In the examples Jesus gave, the bad religious person appears to be living a very holy life

NOT MUCH OF A REWARD!
MAT 6:1-6

(giving, praying and fasting) but he does these things so that others will see and think he is a good person; what a show-off! Instead, Jesus wants His Kingdom people to live a holy life for God, no matter if anyone is watching.

RELIGIOUS LIKE A CHILD OF GOD (6:7-24)

So how can we be religious in a good way? Not with smells, bells and fancy hats ... Rather, we simply put our Father's will first. That's why Jesus starts His prayer with 'Our Father' (v. 9).

Sounds hard, right? Maybe you have had a bad experience with Dads (or maybe never had a Dad), so why should you want to live in a way which pleases our heavenly Dad? One good reason is that He is not like other Dads. Our heavenly Father loves to give good gifts to His children who put Him above all other things – just look at how many times Jesus speaks of our Father rewarding us (vv. 4, 8, 18, 20, 33).

We care for the poor because our Father cares for the poor. We pray because we want to talk to our Father. If we fast (with permission from our parents!) then it should be because we desire to know our Father's will.

SECURE LIKE A CHILD OF GOD (6:25-34)

In Jesus' prayer, we see another great thing about our heavenly Father — we can ask Him for the things we need and then not worry about them (vv. 11–13). Instead of worrying about money, God's children know their Father gives them what they need for life. Instead of holding a grudge against people, God's children can forgive because our Father forgives us. When we are tempted we can turn to our Father who will give us the strength not to sin. God's children never lack God's care!

The world is full of worry and anxiety today, but God's children don't need to be like the world! Look at the promise in verse 33 – if you put the Father's Kingdom first in your to-do list each day, will God ever leave you without His help and care?

EVEN SOLOMON DIDN'T DRESS THIS GOOD!

MAT 6:1-6

QUESTIONS

Being in the Kingdom means not needing to worry. Why not try to find all the different reasons Jesus gives us in verses 25-34 to not worry; these are worth memorising if you get anxious easily!

THE FINAL ASSESSMENT

JUDGING

DISCERNING

Wake up! Jesus is finishing the sermon He started at the beginning of chapter 5, and He is talking about judgement!

ONE JUDGEMENT (7:1-12)

Many people may judge you in life, but there is only one judgement that truly counts: God's judgement. Only God is sinless, so only God can fairly judge sin – you can't do this! However, Jesus does tell us to watch out for sin in others so we can help (v. 5). So what does this look like?

As Jesus said, if you find a sin in someone else, make sure you are not sinning even more than them. You can't help someone take a speck out of their eye if you have a log in yours! In the same way, you can't help someone to stop lying if you

only live like a Christian on Sunday mornings. But if you are right with God, He will help you be discerning and helpful.

ONE CHOICE TO MAKE (7:13-23)

When God's judgement does come, for some it will be good news and for others it will be terrifying. This is no laughing matter! Jesus tells us that one of two things will happen: if we are in God's Kingdom, then King Jesus takes any danger or judgement we face on this last day. The King keeps us totally safe. But if we reject the King, there is nobody to keep us safe and we have to face judgement alone, a scary thought. So who will you trust in, Jesus or yourself?

ONE FOUNDATION (7:24-29)

Did you know that every action you do is because of a thought you already had? Who is shaping those thoughts in your head? Jesus tells us to listen carefully to Him, to trust Him and to obey Him so that you can make good decisions in life. Remember: Jesus wants the best for you! If we don't listen to Him, we are building our life upon sand. And like a grain of sand, the best wisdom of the world may look pretty solid when you pick it up, but if you sit on a beach which is full of it, you will eventually be washed away.

Instead, Jesus and His words are not sand – they are solid rock. Even when God judges the world, someone who lives on this rock will never wash away. Open your Bible today! Its full of rock hard words of the King, secure for a lifetime of building.

QUESTIONS

Remember: the best time to start building a house is yesterday, the second best time is today – how will you build your life upon Jesus today (v. 24)?

CRIKEY!

MAT 7:24-25

LIFE IN THE KINGDOM

TOUCHING THE UNTOUCHABLE (8:1-4)

Can you imagine nobody ever wanting to touch you, or even come near to you? Never mind being unpopular at school, suffering from leprosy in Jesus' time meant that you were banished from society. Your body would slowly become dead and numb, while at the same time, you couldn't speak to anyone you knew or even go into the Jewish temple. Horrible!

Despite all this, when this man suffering from leprosy showed faith in the power of our King, Jesus was not concerned about what people thought. He *touched* the man, healing him instantly and allowing him to enter back into society. Jesus was wonderfully *able* and *willing* to heal.

Sin is a disease much like leprosy in Jesus' time. If it's not dealt with, it slowly destroy us and keeps us out of God's Kingdom. The leprous man was only made 'clean' again by going to the Jewish priest. In the same way, we are only made clean by going to our priest (Jesus) and repenting (remember 3:1-6?). Even though Christians need to keep on repenting from sin, God has counted us clean, once and for all. Like the man cured of leprosy, we can be welcomed back into His society – into His Kingdom.

THE AUTHORITY OF THE KING (8:5-13)

After Jesus finished His message on the mountainside, the crowds were astonished by the authority with which He spoke. How could He be more

JUST HIS WORD IS ENOUGH TO COMMAND HEALING!

THE EMPEROR →

ME! →

J

(ONLY POWERFUL PEOPLE GET TO WEAR HATS AS SILLY AS THIS) →

are forgiven! So what is this great trust the officer had in verse 10? Jesus calls it faith.

THE MESSIAH OF HEALING (5:14-17)

To the Jews (remember, Matthew is writing to ancient Jews!) a leprosy sufferer, a non-Jewish Roman and a woman would all have been counted as *second class* citizens – you just don't mix with them. But in Jesus' Kingdom there is no such category. Anyone can be a part of His Kingdom no matter what problems you are dealing with. Does a physical or social difficulty leave you feeling like an outsider today? It is to people like you that Jesus opens the Kingdom's doors; come on in!

powerful than the Jewish leaders? Well, Jesus wasn't finished yet ...

Next, an important military leader of about 100 men amazingly humbles himself before Jesus. The centurion could see what none of the Jewish leaders could see: Jesus has so much authority that simply by speaking, the world changes, evil is destroyed, people are healed and sins

QUESTIONS

- When God's Kingdom is finally established, all sickness and pain will be healed. How does Matthew 8:1-17 help you trust that Jesus has the power and authority to do this?

- How does Matthew 8:1-17 help you trust that Jesus wants to do this?

WHAT SORT OF PERSON IS THIS?

FOLLOWING JESUS (8:18–22)

If Jesus was walking about performing miracles today, He would be surrounded by people wanting to get close to Him – not to mention all the paparazzi! But following Jesus means much more than simply seeing what He does or even saying 'I am a Christian.' It costs!

respect our parents (John 19:25–29; Exodus 20:12), but if commitment to family means that we cannot follow Jesus, we must reorder our priorities. (Remember, Jesus loves your family way more than you do!)

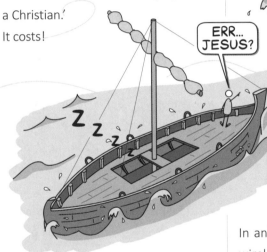

ERR... JESUS?

For the first man who approached Jesus in this passage it would cost him his comfortable lifestyle. Even that night, Jesus was sleeping in a boat on stormy seas rather than in a warm, dry bed.

The second man felt pressure to put family first. As we see elsewhere, Jesus loves family and the Ten Commandments tell us to

WEATHER AND DEMONS (8:22–34)

In an age of self-driving vehicles and wireless toasters you might think our technology can do anything! However, even today, humans are still powerless when it comes to weather and we have little understanding of spiritual evil.

But Jesus is not defeated by any obstacle. He can cure every disease, He can give the sea a telling-off (and it listens!), and even 100 demons are forced to obey Jesus' command. It is no wonder His disciples ask

JESUS, I'D LIKE TO FOLLOW YOU BUT FIRST I NEED TO GET GOOD GRADES, BE POPULAR, GET A BOYFRIEND, CHOOSE A CAREER, GET MARRIED, SETTLE DOWN, GET A CAT HAVE SOME KIDS, GET THEM OFF TO SCHOOL, SORT OUT A PENSION, MOVE HOUSE...

the question: 'What kind of man is this?' (8:27).

THE GREATEST ENEMY (9:1-8)

The angel in chapter one told us that Jesus came to save His people from their sins – a problem so big, *only* God can deal with it. So when Jesus openly forgives the sins of the paralysed man in 9:1–8, the Jewish teachers nearly have a heart attack; surely Jesus wasn't implying that *He* was God? Well, that's exactly what Jesus was implying, but this wasn't blasphemy, He really is God!

And He can prove it. Jesus is so powerful and has so much authority that He makes a paralysed man walk

by simply commanding him – this is something only God's power could do! Jesus argues if He can do that then surely He is also able to forgive sin in the same way God forgives sin.

If you ever doubt that Jesus has forgiven the sins you repent of, just look at this passage. Even though you can't *see* anything happen when you are forgiven does not mean it hasn't happened!

WHAT KIND OF MAN IS JESUS?
TEACHER! 8:19 YES... AND?
LORD! 8:21 YES AND?
BLASPHEMER!!! 9:3
...OOOH SO CLOSE

QUESTIONS

What things might you put before Jesus? (Family, friends, money, success, comfort, entertainment, etc.) Pray that God would help you put Jesus first.

What needs to change in your daily life to show that Jesus gets the top spot?

THE NEW HAS COME

THE DOCTOR IS HERE (9:9-13)

Imagine a known bully became teacher's pet in your class. You would probably feel really mad that such a horrid person was treated so well by a teacher. However, that feeling would be nothing compared to how a Jew would feel when they found out Jesus chose a *tax collector* to be His disciple. Tax collectors were a rotten bunch who would cheat people of their money ... and they worked for the Romans. No self-respecting Jew liked the Romans. So why did Jesus come for a tax collector like Matthew?

As Jesus says, He did not come for the perfect religious people of the world; He came for the sick. The Jewish leaders didn't think they were sick sinners, and so they didn't think they needed healing from Jesus. But Matthew was different. He may have been an untrustworthy and greedy tax collector, even one of the worst, but He knew He was sick and needed healing. Quick! Call for Jesus the Doctor!

FEASTING, NOT FASTING (9:14-17)

The Pharisees fasted. John the Baptist's disciples fasted. But Jesus' disciples ... they were feasting! Why?

One day, when Jesus returns (more about this later) we are told there will be a wedding between Jesus (the 'bridegroom') and His church, the 'bride'. When you spend time with the bridegroom at a wedding, nobody is sad and nobody is fasting. It's the same with Jesus. The disciples were

NOW, DON'T TELL ANYONE ABO—

WE'RE HEALED!

MAT 9:30-31

standing right next to Him; this was a time for eating and celebration!

Today, Jesus is physically ruling in heaven, so Christians wait and fast until Jesus the bridegroom finally returns. Just like Christians in the New Testament, we do this full of joy and anticipation because one day the whole church will join God's table at a huge wedding feast (9:15, Rev. 19:6–9).

BAD BITTERNESS (9:18-34)

Isn't this passage exciting? Jesus has come to heal the sick, to call sinful people (like us) into His Kingdom and to get us ready for a wedding feast. Death is defeated, sight is given, mouths are opened and demons are given the boot – sounds pretty good, right?

And yet, the religious leaders aren't interested, they are grumbling in a corner while everyone else celebrates. They don't want this amazing King; they want to be in charge! Such bitterness leads to a terrible thing – they accuse God of working with Satan (9:34). If only they could see this good Doctor who offers a feast – would they have felt differently?

QUESTIONS

- If you feel bitter about something at church, ask yourself: 'Is the problem with the church or with me?'

- Pray for God's help and read His word (the Bible) to figure your feelings out.

THE HARVEST IS PLENTIFUL 9:37

THOMAS, IT'S AD 29... WHERE ON EARTH DID YOU GET A TRACTOR FROM?!

INTO THE FIELDS (9:35-38)

Martin Luther supposedly said that Christians are like manure: if you spread them out over an area, they can help life grow, but if you pile them up in one place, they begin to stink. In churches today it can be easy to become a 'back-row' Christian; happy to listen but never taking the gospel further than a Sunday morning service. Well, as Luther might have put it, 'That stinks!'

Before now, the disciples have mostly stayed at Jesus' feet, listening and learning. However, now the King sends them out to work as farmers. He can see what we can't; the fields of people in the world are filled with those who are ripe and ready to respond to the message of the Kingdom. We shouldn't think it's any different today. We can't tell who is going to respond to our good news but, if we simply obey Jesus' instruction, we get to be part of this cultivation sensation!

BECAUSE OF ME (10:1-25)

Jesus does not mince His words: this farming expedition will be tough. Whole homes and towns will reject the message (10:14), the disciples will be arrested and physically punished by the authorities (10:17), and they will be chased about by people who want them dead (10:21–23)! But all this wasn't because of who the disciples were, but rather, because of who their King was (10:25).

DON'T BE AFRAID (10:26-42)

When we read that along with all this, being a Christian means that your own family may turn against you, we may want to shrink back. But throughout this section, Jesus gives His farmers a number of reasons to be fearless.

If you are frightened nobody will listen to you, don't worry, you are only responsible to share the message; you're not responsible for how people respond (10:12–13).

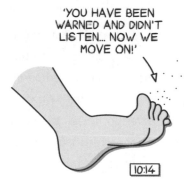

'YOU HAVE BEEN WARNED AND DIDN'T LISTEN... NOW WE MOVE ON!'

10:14

If you fear about not having the right words to say, don't worry, the Holy Spirit, God Himself, will give you the words you need (10:19–20).

If you fear others will twist things to make you look like you are doing wrong, don't worry, God will one day reveal such lies for what they are (10:25–26).

If you fear listeners may turn on you, even to kill you, Jesus says, 'do not be afraid' (v. 28). Even death is like nothing when compared to the perfect peace and joy of heaven (Rom. 8:18). God, who cares for His people, is in charge of our body and souls. Do we have any reason to be afraid of people who can only affect the body?

QUESTIONS

What stops you sharing Jesus' Kingdom message with others?

Looking at this passage, what does Jesus say to you in response?

WHAT DID YOU EXPECT?

MESSIAH AHEAD

MISSING THE SIGNS (11:1-6)

Did you know? Even faithful people can have doubts about Jesus. In chapter 3, John the Baptist was preaching about the coming King Jesus with great gusto! But now he is in prison (see chapter 14) and full of doubts about everything he had been saying. What had happened? He had missed all the signs.

In the Bible, miracles are always signs pointing us to God. That's their main job! So when Jesus sends a reply to John, He lists all the miracles He has been performing (v. 5). Amazingly, the miracles Jesus had performed all appear in the book of Isaiah, written 700 years beforehand (check out Isaiah 35, for example). Isaiah had predicted that God would one day come amongst His people to judge and to save. By doing the miracles Isaiah expected, Jesus proves that day finally has arrived.

IGNORING THE MESSENGER (11:7-15)

Jesus then points to another prophecy to help prove His case. He says that God promised someone would prepare Israel for the arrival of a King (v. 10). As we have already seen, this man was John the Baptist, calling people from miles around to repent!

Israel had heard a messenger like this before. In the Old Testament, the prophet Elijah turned Israel back from faithlessness to instead worship God. In verses 13–14, Jesus explains that John was just like Elijah, preparing God's people for the Kingdom about to arrive. Both have the same Kingdom message: 'Turn back to God!' If someone says to you, 'the God of the Old Testament is different from the God of the New Testament', here is a great place to show them that's just not true – God's messengers have always had the same message!

PLAYING A GAME (11:16-19)

In response to such evidence, the crowds played the 'what-about' game. The rules are simple: when someone presents you with evidence which shows Jesus is King, bring up an unrelated reason to question them!

For example: the crowd thought John's fasting behaviour meant he had a demon, so they ignored His message. But when Jesus ate food, they accused Him of being a greedy sinner! No matter what Jesus did, people would find a reason to ignore Him.

This game still goes on today. Even if you present all the evidence in the world, some people will pay no attention and ask 'well, what about ...' But don't worry; they did the same thing to Jesus.

QUESTIONS

If you could prove Jesus is God and King, would everyone believe you? (Jn 3:5-8). Think about how this changes the way you tell people about Jesus.

ONLY BY THE SON

KNOWING THE KING (11:20-30)

If you wanted to meet the Queen, you probably wouldn't just hop the fence at Buckingham Palace, walk up to the front door and say to the guards with the fluffy hats, 'just popping in to see Her Majesty!' (That would not end well for you.) But many people think we can access God, the King of the whole universe, with even less effort – just by praying!

Of course, for a Christian, the amazing thing is we *can* speak to God simply by praying ... but who let us into the throne room of the King?

In verse 27, Jesus tells us something absolutely mind-blowing: nobody can know God the Father unless God the Son chooses to reveal Him. This job can only be carried out by Jesus. As we will see later on, it's only by Jesus' work on earth that we can gain access to God, it's only by Jesus' continuing work today that we can speak to God and it's only by Jesus' sacrifice that we can one day live with God. So if Jesus is the only way, how should we come to Him?

TWO WAYS TO APPROACH

The first option is the crazy Buckingham Palace approach – just find your own way through. Jesus performed lots of miracles (or signs) in certain towns (v. 21) but still many people ignored Him as the way to God. Such people may appear wise (v. 25), but Jesus tells us that the true way to God will be hidden from them and they will be judged harshly (vv. 20-24).

'TRYING TO MAKE GOD LIKE ME BY DOING GOOD THINGS'

1 TON
RELIGIOUS RULES

The second option is to approach the only way that makes sense: as a little child who needs the care of their Father to survive. Like in a good father-child relationship, the

Dad only asks for obedience, but the child is given everything!

The Jewish leaders at the time asked for more than obedience, they wanted the people to do even more than what God asks for. This burden (or yoke) was placed upon God's people and it weighed them down (vv. 28–30). We might feel the same about the burdens of everyday life, but Jesus tells us that His yoke is something rather special; living as Jesus wants us to is not only light, it actually lifts us up! Now that's a weight off your shoulders!

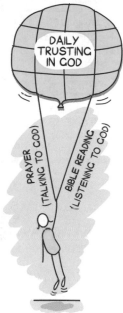

DAILY TRUSTING IN GOD

PRAYER (TALKING TO GOD)

BIBLE READING (LISTENING TO GOD)

QUESTIONS

What burdens are you hanging on to? If you seek Jesus first, His burden will give you rest.

How do you approach God in prayer? Remember this privilege was only made possible by Jesus.

THE WORD OF LAW

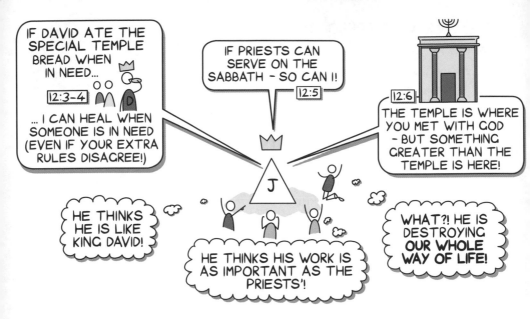

GREATER THAN THE TEMPLE (12:1-6)

Nothing was more important to first-century Jewish leaders than the temple and the Sabbath. These religious things were designed to please God but the leaders used them as a way to look good. When Jesus reminds them that the true purpose of God's laws and God's temple was to show their need of a saviour, and not their goodness, the religious leaders get very angry.

And we can see why! In just a few lines, Jesus causes them great offence, He says:

Believe it or not, it is very easy to make the same mistake as the Jewish leaders; we too can be tempted to think that religious activity is more important than living as the King wants us to. For example, have you ever become proud of your good attendance at church or youth group and showed this off to your friends? If so, check your heart! Our words should not make others feel bad about church involvement. Instead, they should point others to the One whom church is all about.

THE HEART OF THE LAW (12:7–14)

We see this when Jesus tells us the heart of the law is not to measure how good a Christian you are but to show the mercy and love of God (v. 7). It is incredible, when Jesus heals a man of his disabled arm all the Pharisees cared about is that He did it on the Sabbath! In fact, the Jewish leaders are so enraged by Jesus' selfless actions that they start planning how to kill Him.

THE SUFFERING SERVANT (12:15–21)

When Jesus becomes aware of these murderous plans, He leaves the area and Matthew then shows us another Old Testament prophecy being fulfilled.

Isaiah spoke of a suffering Servant of God, and He looks just like Jesus. He would come to bring justice to the world (v. 18) and He would care for bruised people; people who feel like a candle about to be snuffed out (v. 20). For now, this Servant has not come to argue and cause a scene in the streets (v. 19), but one day, He will cause the biggest scene the world has ever known: intense suffering leading to victory for His people.

LOVE, MERCY, COMPASSION

LORD OF THE SABBATH (HE IS IN CHARGE)

J

SABBATH REST TO: MY PEOPLE

SOME RULES

E.G. DT 5:12–15

MORE RULES = MORE HOLY!

PHARISEES

RULES

E.G. MARK 7:1–8

GOD'S PEOPLE

MAT 11:28 J NO MORE! COME TO ME NOT THE PHARISEES, I WILL GIVE YOU REST

QUESTIONS

God desires mercy, not sacrifice (v. 7).

How would someone tell that you are a Christian?

Is it because you go to church or is it because your daily behaviour shows kindness and compassion?

TWO KINGDOMS COLLIDE

Have you ever noticed that on TV the church and its people are often painted as the 'bad guy'? This is not a coincidence, the same thing happens to Jesus in this passage. If people cannot deny the miracles of Jesus, the next form of attack is to accuse Him (or His followers) of doing evil. The battle of the kingdoms continues ...

JESUS' KINGDOM (12:22–32)

When the Pharisees saw Jesus send another demon packing (v. 22), they accused Him of working for Satan's kingdom. You should know, Satan ('the Devil') is powerful – John 12:31 and 14:30 describe him as the ruler of this world! But this accusation was ridiculous. As Jesus points out, why on earth would Satan want to banish his own demons? If a kingdom attacks its own people, it will destroy itself.

Instead, the Pharisees should have seen what was really going on: God's Kingdom was destroying Satan's worldly power. We have already seen this when Jesus defeated Satan in the wilderness (4:1–11) and now we find out that Satan has been bound up like a prisoner so that anyone trapped by his power can be set free (v. 29). Did you think being a Christian was boring? No way! Christian's follow their King into battle: rescuing captives to sin, defeating works of evil and speaking truth against the enemy's lies.

SATAN'S KINGDOM (12:33-37)

Jesus returns fire against the Pharisees: a King can only fight for his own side, and a tree can only bear its own type of fruit. The fruit of the Pharisees tells us that they have Satan as their King. What does this fruit look

...BUT JESUS DEFEATS THEM SIMPLY BY SPEAKING!
MAT 8:32 15:28 17:18
(TALK TO YOUR PASTOR IF THESE THINGS WORRY YOU)

like? It looks like asking for more and more 'signs' for Jesus to prove who He is, despite plenty of evidence given already (v. 38), it looks like twisting

the truth (v. 24), it looks like refusing to accept the Holy Spirit is at work (vv. 30–32) and it looks like a refusal to turn away from sins (v. 41). Mouldy, black, dead fruit.

UNDER THE CROWN (12:38-50)

Jesus tells us something very important about these Kingdoms at the end of our passage (vv. 46–50). We are not born into a Kingdom; we enter them through obeying a King. Being a son or daughter of Christian parents does not make you a Christian: living in obedience to King Jesus does. In the same way, being a son or daughter of unbelieving parents does not make you an enemy of God: living like you are your own King or Queen does.

QUESTIONS

Both Kingdoms are active today in words and supernatural power.

- How will you be able to identify the works of God or the works of Satan? (See I John 4:2-6.)

THE FOUR REACTIONS TO THE KINGDOM

Did you know, when you tell someone about God's Kingdom, you will only ever see one of four reactions? In this parable, Jesus describes the Christian as a farmer and those who hear their message as different types of soil.

THE PAVED SOIL (13:18-19)

This can be hard to take, but some people will simply stop listening when you talk about Jesus. Like a hard path, the heart of such a person is solid as rock — nothing can get into it. It's only by prayer that any change will happen. God must give this soil new ears to hear, new eyes to see and a new heart to love Jesus — just like He gave you.

Of course, Christians can be totally deaf sometimes as well. Sometimes we can come to church on a Sunday and leave our brains at the front door; no thinking and no praying involved! Bad move. After being spoken, God's truth does not stay lying about; Satan is quick to snatch up the seed we don't take in.

THE ROCKY SOIL (13:20-21)

NOPE, NOT INTERESTED!

BOINK!

PING!

Sometimes those who initially get very excited about Jesus will leave Him when the going gets tough. Often they have not fully understood that being a

Christian is not all fun and games, it can be really hard. For many people, the cost of family or friends rejecting them because of their new Christian faith is a price too high to pay.

THE THORNY SOIL (13:22)

It is so easy to get distracted by things in life instead of following Jesus. These can be things we

enjoy like getting good grades or earning money, or it can simply be the problems of daily life like doing homework or chores. Nobody likes weeding the lawn (unless you're a bit odd) but if you never get your gardening fork out, distractions will grow and slowly pull you away from God.

THE GOOD SOIL (13:23)

When someone truly understands who Jesus is, this truth goes deep into their very being. Not only will

they say 'I am a Christian' but the seed in them gives growth in every aspect of their lives. In fact, the best way to spot good soil is to see if it produces more seeds (v. 23) – when you get to know Jesus, it can be very hard not to tell other people about Him!

QUESTIONS

Don't give up on someone because they appear to be one type of soil or another. How can you best pray for people you know who appear to be each type of soil?

Think back to how people have reacted to Jesus so far in Matthew: what type of soils can you see?

THE KINGDOM OF HEAVEN IS LIKE ...

THE KINGDOM CO-EXISTS (13:24-30)

Hold on a minute ... if the King has arrived (4:17) and has tied up the enemy (12:29), then why does the world today still look like there has been no real victory over evil? People get ill and die, crime and pain still exists – has the King abandoned us?

The parable of the weeds tells us not to be surprised that evil is still in the world because members of Satan's Kingdom are still in the world. According to the parable, there will come a time when God will separate His Kingdom people from Satan's, but until then we will suffer for a short time. Why the wait? It's not because God doesn't love us, but because God *does* love us! His people (the wheat) is so precious, He won't risk damaging their growth by ripping up Satan's weeds.

Until the time is right, both plants exist together (v. 29).

THE KINGDOM SHALL GROW LARGE (13:31-43)

However, despite being surrounded by weeds, the Kingdom is not stunted in growth. Just like a tiny mustard seed produces a tree large enough to fill a garden; the Kingdom of Heaven will one day fill the world.

The disciples would have been especially glad to hear this. Can you imagine being one of only twelve Christians on the planet and being told it was your job to spread the Kingdom message? Talk about being dropped in at the deep end! Thankfully, when we feel weak and helpless in such

a big task, we can look back to these faithful few and see how God brings about huge growth from the smallest of beginnings.

TAP TAP

THE KINGDOM IS PRICELESS (13:44–52)

If those in the Kingdom will one day be *joyfully* gathered into God's barn and will one day *joyfully* fill the earth, then guess what it feels like to be given access to this Kingdom … joyful! In his joy, the man who found treasure in a field sold every single thing he owned so that he could possess the Kingdom of Heaven. To grab hold of the Kingdom, we may need to leave behind being popular, having

'cool' stuff, getting the best grades, having a certain boyfriend or girlfriend … but Jesus tells us these things are no sacrifice in comparison. If you need to give these up, you are swapping them for something even more precious – everlasting life with Jesus!

QUESTIONS

- What would hurt the most to leave behind in order to keep following Jesus?
- How does this passage give you comfort that God will make it well worth the cost?

47

MIRACLES OF THE KING

TWO FEASTS (13:53-14:21)

What's the difference between Satan's Kingdom and Jesus' Kingdom (13:24–29; 36–43; 47–50)? We can tell by looking at their meal times.

In 14:1-12, the rich and powerful are gathering around a banquet at the palace of Herod (the son of the Herod in Matthew 1 – neither of them were nice guys). At this feast, it looks like Herod's daughter-in-law was forced to dance seductively in front of Herod's dinner guests. When offered a reward, she asked for her Mum's advice. Her Mum (who also wasn't particularly nice, and hated John the Baptist) told her to demand John's head on a plate. Pretty sick, right? But this is a perfect picture of Satan's Kingdom: everyone interested in satisfying their own desires, and the result is death.

Jesus' feast is different. In 14:13-21 we see the poor and needy of the world coming to the King and given wholesome food. Instead of dark parties, there is healing. Instead of self-satisfaction, even the poorest are satisfied by Jesus. There is so much need, but Jesus easily provides more than required! And look, the result of this meal is totally different: Jesus is shown to be loving and powerful, and absolutely everyone has a full belly (14:20). What meal would you rather attend?

STORMY STEPS (14:22-36)

Jesus is just like the God who rescued Israel from Egypt (because He is

God!) and He rescues His people from being slaves (to sin, not an Egyptian Pharaoh, remember what He said in Matthew 1:21). With powerful miracles He fed them in a wilderness place (14:13–21, like Israel in the desert) and now we see He even controls the sea like the God of Jewish history (8:23–27; 14:25–29). Surely by now the disciples have learned to simply trust in God for everything?

Thankfully, when we get into a similar situation, we can do exactly what Peter did – cry out 'Lord, save me!' You will see in verse 31, *immediately* Jesus reached out His hand and caught Peter. The Lord does not leave His children in troubled waters and God is no slower in reaching out His hand to catch us today (even if we can't see it at first).

BYE, GUYS

SIMON PETER – WHAT ARE YOU LIKE

Nope! In the middle of a storm, Peter certainly trusts enough that he is willing to step onto a raging sea, but as doubts slowly creep in, the disciple begins to sink down below the waves. Perhaps he thought 'How could a good God be calling me into such a storm?' or, 'With all the waves and trouble around me, how can I possibly keep afloat?'

QUESTIONS

When the storms of life happen, how do you react?

Seek help from God or try to fight on without Jesus?

DIRTY HANDS, CLEAN HEARTS

GOD VS TRADITION (15:1-9)

Did you know, God thinks honouring your parents is so important that He put it in His Ten Commandments (Exodus 20:12)? This not only means obeying your parents when you are young, but helping your parents when they get old.

The big-shot Pharisees from Jerusalem certainly *did* know that, but over the years they had developed a sneaky system where they could keep all their wealth without having to spend it on looking after old parents. By taking a vow which said 'all my wealth belongs to God', the Pharisees could actually store up money for themselves in the temple. On the outside, this might have looked very holy, but in reality their 'donated' wealth was merely selfish hoarding.

This sounds pretty horrible, but we should be careful in pointing the finger. Have you ever used church events or the Pastor's sermon as an excuse to disobey your parents? Jesus is very clear here, nobody can use traditions or teaching outside of the Bible to avoid doing God's will.

THE JEWISH LEADERS THOUGHT BEING CLEAN MADE GOD'S PEOPLE STAND OUT...

BUT JESUS' FOLLOWERS SHOULD STAND OUT IN A DIFFERENT WAY

JOHN 13:35

FROM THE HEART! (15:10-20)

When the disciples didn't wash their hands before eating, it violated extra rules that the Pharisees had added on to Old Testament commands. As far as they were concerned, the disciples were now religiously 'unclean' and so could not enter into the temple or be accepted by God.

However, they have it wrong – again. The Pharisees thought extra rules made them extra holy, but this isn't right at all! Jesus quotes from Isaiah to show that rules exist to help God's people match their hearts' desire with God's. God's laws are designed to give us a heart like Jesus'.

Jesus then explains, it's not what goes into a person that 'defiles' them, but it is what comes out of a persons' heart. In other words, nobody is rejected by God because of something they have eaten or because of a past bad experience, but we will all be measured by what our heart produces.

FOOD

EVIL WORDS

EVIL! BIG PROBLEM

NO EVIL, NO PROBLEM

EVIL ACTIONS

If you are not a Christian, your hard heart will cause you to do and say things which show you are not right before God. However, if you are a Christian, God has given you a new heart (Ezekiel 36:26). As a result you can love God, do good, and honour Him with words and actions.

BUT MUM! THE DISCIPLES DIDN'T WASH THEIR HANDS!

IF A DISCIPLE BETRAYED JESUS, WOULD YOU DO THAT TOO?!

QUESTIONS

- Thank God that He gives you a new heart to make you right before Him.

- Are special religious rules always bad? (For example, is making a rule to pray at the same time each day a bad thing?)

- Do these activities make you right before God or do they lead you to God?

THIS KINGDOM IS GOING TO THE DOGS

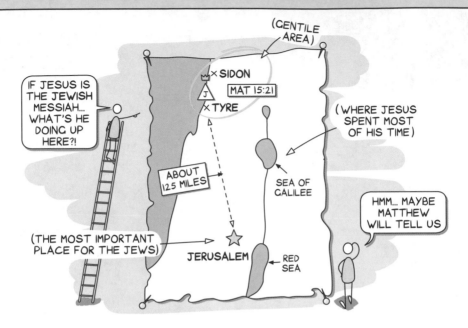

THE GOSPEL SPREADS (15:21)

Throughout history, God has always had a special place for His chosen people, the Jews (Deuteronomy 7:6; Romans 1:16). However, Jesus goes well beyond the Jewish cities into Gentile (non-Jewish) territory. God's Kingdom is expanding to bring in people from all over the world!

NO, NO, NO, YES (15:22-28)

On Jesus' travels He is met by a Gentile mother who wants help for her daughter. And as you may have noticed: Jesus calls that woman a dog. (Not the kind of verse you see on a Christian fridge magnet!)

This would be shocking today, but was this word offensive to the woman? Probably not; Bible experts think Jesus was using it in a clever way. Jesus wasn't insulting the woman, but helping her put her faith into words.

"It is not right to take the children's bread and toss it to the dogs"

The woman got three 'no's for her requests. First, she cries out for help from the King, the 'Son of David', but she got *no answer*. Then, the disciples wanted Jesus to heal her daughter ... but only so the woman would stop bothering them! They were also told 'no'. Then, the woman came kneeling before Jesus and was told 'no' directly; Jesus had come first to the Jews, not for Gentiles like her.

THANKS, DOES HE DO SALT AND VINEGAR?

But finally, even though the woman knew Jesus owed her nothing, she cries out for healing. And, because she trusted in Jesus' mercy, she is given what she doesn't deserve; her daughter is healed.

Most of us reading this story will be Gentiles also. So when Jesus accepts us into His Kingdom, we are also getting something first promised to Jews only, but given to us by God's grace. Amazing!

DÉJÀ VU (15:29-39)

Hold on ... Bread and fish? Clueless disciples? Thousands of people fed by a miracle? We have seen this before! Why is Matthew telling us another miraculous feeding story?

It's because Matthew wants to make something really clear: Jesus

is bringing hope to the Gentiles. The Jews didn't think the Gentile people were worth much at the time (that's why the Jews called them 'dogs'), but Jesus thinks otherwise. He opens up His invitation and power to anyone who comes to Him in faith, no matter who they are. This is true equality. Jesus has come for all outsiders, even you today!

QUESTIONS

- This woman kept being told 'no' by Jesus, but her faith actually grew stronger each time she asked for help. Are your prayers sometimes like this?

- Anyone who trusts in Jesus as their King is a part of His Kingdom – even the most unlikely people. Who is unlikely out of your friends to trust in Jesus? Pray that God would help them see Jesus like this woman did.

AN IDENTIFICATION REVELATION

SEEING POORLY (16:1-4)

It might seem obvious, but when we come to speak to God, He is God and we are merely human. (I said it was obvious ...) But look at how the Pharisees approach Jesus in verse 1; have they forgotten how to be humble?

On the surface, their request seems harmless, right? If Jesus would simply perform one little miracle, *then* they would believe He is the Messiah ... is this not a good thing to ask? No! This kind of testing is so dangerous!

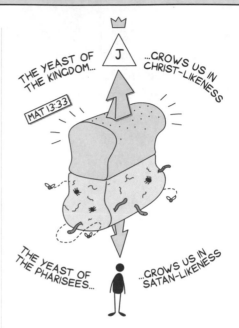

THE YEAST OF THE KINGDOM...

MAT 13:33

...GROWS US IN CHRIST-LIKENESS

THE YEAST OF THE PHARISEES...

...GROWS US IN SATAN-LIKENESS

HOW DO YOU APPROACH KING JESUS?

The Pharisees have already seen Jesus perform *hundreds* of miracles, they have heard Him teach wisdom *far* better than they knew how, and they have heard His Kingdom message of repentance and forgiveness *many* times – what more do they want?

Their demand for a sign is not from a heart searching for God, but from a heart that wants to control God. They would only believe if God did exactly what they asked!

EATING POORLY (16:5-12)

Do people act like this today? You bet, but they might use nicer words: 'If only God would do *this*, then I would trust in Him ... show me a sign!'

When we ask for this sort of proof, we are actually judging God and have become mixed with the yeast of the Pharisees and Sadducees (v. 6). Yeast makes bread rise but bad yeast makes bad bread!

Jesus warns His disciples of this kind of thinking because someone who needs personalised proof from God will never accept Him as their King. And unless Jesus is our King, we will never be allowed into the Kingdom.

SPEAKING WELL (16:13-20)

Astoundingly, none of the smart Jewish teachers could see who Jesus was, but an uneducated fisherman from the outskirts of nowhere saw that Jesus was God's chosen saviour and King of the world. This faith did not come from Simon Peter demanding evidence of Jesus' identity. No, since we first met him, Peter's faith was built upon simple, humble obedience (4:18–20).

This faithful obedience was God-given, and his ability to see Jesus as the Messiah was also a gift from God (not from his brain!). Here, when Jesus sets Peter up as the leading disciple of the early church, it's based purely upon Peter's God-given faith in Jesus as King. Who cares if you are not the smartest or the strongest person around, if God has given you faith, that's all you need to serve Him fully.

WHO KNEW JESUS BETTER?

ONE FAITHFUL FISHERMAN OR ALL THE KNOWLEDGE OF THE PHARISEES?

QUESTIONS

- The Pharisees were strong, important individuals and very intelligent. Peter caught fish for a living and often got simple things very wrong. So why did Jesus choose to give Peter a position of leadership?

- What type of person does Jesus want as His disciple?

55

THE SECRET MISSION

MISSION IMPOSSIBLE (16:20-21)

Movie heroes never have a mission where the main objective is to die – it would make for a very short film. But dying is central to Jesus' mission. Can you imagine the shock of reading this for the first time? This is our hero! This is God's chosen King coming to save His people! What on earth has suffering and dying got to do with anything?

NO WAY (16:22-23)

That's exactly what went through Peter's head when he heard Jesus' words and so he gives Jesus a telling

off (just like Jesus 'rebuked' the waves in chapter 8!). Yikes! Peter had obviously forgotten this was God he was speaking to; what had got into him?

But it's not 'what' got into him, but *who*! When Jesus responds to Peter, He calls Peter 'Satan' – it was the devil's ideas that had got into him! Like the rest of the Jews, Peter didn't want a Messiah who saves from sins (1:21). Peter wanted a warrior King who would help Israel kick out the Romans – death did not enter into

that picture. Peter wanted what we all want: peace, comfort, and victory in all things! But the problem is: Peter wanted them his own way, just like Satan wanted Jesus to do things his own way in chapter 4.

FIRST THE KING, THEN YOU (16:24-28)

The King has said that He 'must' die (v. 21) and *therefore His Kingdom subjects must also die* (v. 24).

Nobody wants to die, especially not on a cross. But Jesus repeats His warning from 10:38 that unless we are willing to put His Kingdom above even life itself, we cannot follow Him. This means Christians often don't get what they want. In fact, it means giving up many things we do want ('denying yourself')

But the King also said He must 'be raised to life' (v. 21) and *therefore His Kingdom subjects must also be raised to life*.

Hallelujah! Losing the whole world but being raised from the dead is not a hard trade. Even losing everything good in life, but having Jesus as your King means you are rich beyond measure. Jesus' promise to

His disciples is still true for you today: when you one day meet Jesus face to face, there will be *nothing* you regret giving up for Him.

PICKING UP YOUR CROSS...

...MAY MEAN DROPPING SOMETHING ELSE

QUESTIONS

Why did Jesus command them not to tell anyone He was the Messiah? (Consider Peter's mixed understanding on this point – 16:16 and 16:21-22.)

What parts of life do you struggle to give up for Jesus' sake, what things do you still count more important than Him?

Why not let them go and instead have a huge reward in heaven (v. 27)?

BEHIND THE CURTAIN

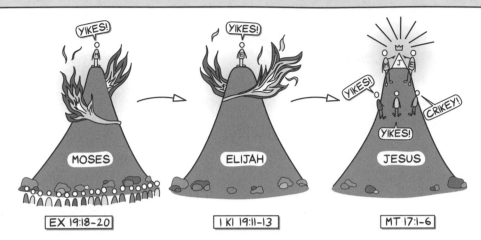

EX 19:18-20 | 1 KI 19:11-13 | MT 17:1-6

THREE ON STAGE (17:1-4)

After a painful discussion in yesterday's passage, the disciples needed some cheering up. As hinted at in 16:28, Jesus is going to show them something important: even though the world can be a hard, painful place, Jesus' Kingdom is a place of life and wonder.

Moses and Elijah are two of the greatest men of the Old Testament and both of them spoke to God on a mountain. Moses spoke with God on Mount Sinai after leading the Israelites out of slavery – on that mountain, Moses' face shone like Jesus' shines here (Exodus 34:29–30). Elijah spoke to God on Mount Horeb – there the Lord encouraged and guided Elijah (1 Kings 19). Moses, a writer of law; Elijah, a prophet ... God had worked through both these great men under the Old Covenant. Now He was doing even more through Jesus in the New Covenant.

This staggering realisation is why Peter's first reaction was to build a shelter for the three great men. But as

Luke points out in his account, Peter was doing a *classic* Peter – all action and little thought (Luke 9:33)!

THE VOICE FROM ABOVE (17:5)

Before Peter got a sentence out, God speaks. Usually when that happens in the Bible, everything else stops and people fall over! Similar to the fire at Mount Sinai and Mount Horeb, a bright cloud appears. Things have reached a climax and now Jesus is centre stage (just like in 3:17!).

This Jesus is the Son of God and King that Israel had been waiting for since they read Psalm 2! *Jesus* is the suffering servant who God the Father loves (Isaiah 42:1). Yes, Moses and Elijah are both big deals – but nothing compared to Jesus! The whole of the Old Testament pointed to His arrival, and now that He's here God's message is very simple: 'Listen to Him!' (v. 5).

NO ONE EXCEPT JESUS (17:6-13)

When this experience ends, the disciples are terrified but also amazed. When they are finally brave enough to look up, they see nobody left but Jesus – and that's exactly how God intended it to be for us too! It is in the toughest and scariest moments of life, when we are flat out on the floor before God, that we realise something really important: no matter what life throws at us, ultimately all we need to see us through is Jesus alone. Listen to Him!

THE SON OF MAN

DANIEL 7:13-14

JESUS USES THIS TITLE FOR HIMSELF A LOT! (MAT 8:20; 9:6; 10:23; 11:19...) DANIEL'S VISION TELLS US 'ONE LIKE A SON OF MAN' WOULD BE GIVEN AUTHORITY TO RULE LIKE GOD OVER ALL THE EARTH – AND YET GOD'S PEOPLE REJECTED HIM! (MAT 17:11)

QUESTIONS

Are you feeling down today? For a moment, turn off all your screens and get away from the world. Spend a moment on the mountaintop with Jesus. Think about His glory and greatness. Perhaps catch a glimpse by reading Revelation 1:12-18.

Do you trust your powerful King?

DOWN THE MOUNTAIN

(EVERYONE GETS SUNDAY NIGHT FEELING)

FROM MAJESTY TO MAYHEM (17:14–20)

Nobody likes the Sunday night feeling! (Unless you're a Pastor, perhaps.) All the encouragement of meeting with God's people on a Sunday is replaced with the thoughts of classes you don't want to go to, people you don't want to see and books you don't want to read ... Well, three of the disciples now had the Sunday night feeling times a thousand as they went from the heavenly vision of the mountain down to the mess of life.

They are met by demon possession (which looked like epilepsy, but these are different things), and the disciples lacked faith that God could do anything about it. As a result, Jesus shows His righteous frustration in verse 17; not because of the demon, but because of the disciples' lack of faith.

FROM GRANDEUR TO GRACE (17:22–27)

Up the mountain, the disciples saw that the whole of creation bows to Jesus as King. Now, someone is asking this *King* to pay His share of temple taxes (v. 24)! Do they not know the Son of God certainly does not need to pay taxes? Everything, including temple money, belongs to Him anyway!

How would you respond to such offence? If we get offended easily, then we should look to Jesus for a big lesson in humility. The King of the universe was asked to pay a tax, *and He paid it*! More than this, instead of being offended, our gracious King was more concerned about not *causing* offence (v. 27)!

TAKE YOUR FAITH

The disciples did not have enough faith to help the demon-possessed boy (v. 20). They also couldn't believe Jesus was going to rise from the dead, that's why they are so sad in verse 23. But way back in 14:33 they all believed Jesus was the Son of God, so where did their faith go?

Well, you could say it was left behind at the big moments of Jesus' miracles. It's easy to be faithful when Jesus calms a storm in chapter 14, and it's easy to be faithful when we really *feel* God's presence. But what about the hard times, or in the normal, daily routine? The big moments prove Jesus is unimaginably powerful and deeply cares for us, but if we forget this in the hard moments or the small moments, then we are leaving our faith behind!

Life changes, but God doesn't. So even If your faith is as small as a mustard seed, take it with you; you're going to need the powerful God it points to!

IF YOU HAVE FAITH IN GOD AT MOMENTS LIKE THIS...

...TAKE IT TO MOMENTS LIKE THESE

"FOR I THE LORD DO NOT CHANGE"

MAL 3:6

QUESTIONS

Why do you dread Mondays? Is life so bad that God can't help you through it? Or are you nervous because you are trying to get through the week without God's help?

CHILDREN AND TRIP HAZARDS

With Peter getting special attention from Jesus (16:18) and Jesus talking about dying soon (16:21; 17:22), it looks like the disciples are wondering who is going to be in charge of this group (v. 1)! After all, knowing who is important is, well ... important! But Jesus' answer reminds the disciples that in God's Kingdom, everything is turned upside down.

But we *are* called to be like children. We should think of ourselves as the least important in any group and we are to come to our

GREAT IN GOD'S KINGDOM

DAD! HELP!

STUMBLING HAZARDS

BEING A BIG KID (18:1-5)

Unlike the world, those in the Kingdom must be needy and helpless like a child. From a practical point of view, a child is always the least important member of society. Children cannot get food for themselves or provide for others. They are never the head of companies and they rarely make good Kings. Children are not smart or strong ... actually, the more you think about it, who wants to be a kid?!

heavenly Father for everything, the same way a child needs a parent for everything. Christians can still be rich, smart and important, but remember: none of these things makes you 'great' in God's Kingdom.

REMOVING STUMBLING BLOCKS (18:6-9)

Kingdom people must always be aware of how their behaviour affects themselves and others. Jesus is deadly serious here: if our actions make it harder for others to follow God we should expect to be punished. Sure, mistakes happen; God forgives us if we repent. But if we are willingly and repeatedly the source of sin then something is gravely wrong. We need an emergency operation!

Do your friends cause you to sin? Don't hang out with those friends! Do electronic devices cause you to sin? Don't use them! It's better to only have friends at church (or even no friends!) and be without a cool phone than to be the cause of stumbling.

CARING FOR LOST SHEEP (18:10-14)

Christians should care about people stumbling, but we should also care about people wandering away from God. When one of His flock goes astray, our God is like a good shepherd who will not stop looking for this sheep until it is returned,

then He is filled with joy. Our God loves His sheep, but do we?

When someone leaves church, others might not be worried, but we should care as much as God cares. If your friend is wandering away today, don't add stones for them to trip over should they want to come back to Jesus, instead, make the path clear and bring them home to joyful celebration!

RIGHT, STAY HERE. I'M OFF TO GET LIAM... AGAIN!

THINK HE WAS CHASING A BEE...

OH THAT IS SO LIAM

QUESTIONS

If one of your friends is fed up of God and the church, how can you help them?

WHEN THE RUBBER HITS THE ROAD

You might think living in God's Kingdom would be perfect because Christians should be kind, loving people. However, it turns out everyone else is as messed up and sinful as you are! That's why we need clear instructions on what to do when God's people sin.

COLLECTIVE DISCIPLINE (18:15-19)

Jesus gives us a really easy to follow process. When someone in the church is sinning without repenting of that sin, it is your responsibility to first talk alone with that individual. Not to tell them off or seek revenge (Romans 12:19), but to try and 'win them over' for the sake of the church. If that fails, you should ask for others to help you do this. Finally, if the individual still won't listen, the leaders of the church come together to ask the person to repent. If that person still doesn't turn away from their sin, then the leaders will treat them like an outsider (v. 17).

This is a group exercise. The only single individual at the top of the church is Jesus (Colossians 1:18), He is in charge of church discipline. How is that possible? Thankfully, as suggested

GATHERING IN OUR NAME

GATHERING IN JESUS' NAME

in verses 18–20, when we meet together, Jesus promises His presence with us and grants His approval on resolutions made in His name. This doesn't mean God approves anything we ask for, but it does mean that the Holy Spirit will guide gatherings of Christians when trying to figure these things out through prayer.

PERSONAL FORGIVENESS (18:21-35)

What about when someone sins against you, personally? How many times should you forgive them? Peter thought seven times was an extravagant number, 'surely not more than seven times!' (v. 21). But Jesus reminds Peter that we should forgive the same way God has forgiven us.

The King in Jesus' parable represents God, and the servant represents a person like us. The servant owed the King so much money that he would have to work more than *two hundred thousand years* to pay it back! Really, think about that. The servant, only able to work for sixty years at best, is as far away from paying his debt as we are from paying God back for our sins. Incredibly, the servant's debt was cancelled, yet in his pride,

he still counted the tiny debt owed to him by another servant.

Your debts are forever cancelled; if you are still counting the number of times you need to forgive someone, you have missed the point! Let's forgive like we have been forgiven.

> FORGIVE 490 TIMES?! I NEED TO START KEEPING A LIST!

1 COR 13:4-5

490
70 x 7

QUESTIONS

Read Ephesians 2:1-5 and thank God for His mercy. If God has done all this for you, even though you are a sinner, how will you respond when wronged by others?

VALUE AND COMMITMENT

EPH 5:25

THE VALUE OF MARRIAGE (19:1–12)

In the time of the disciples, marriages were abused much like they are today; many people did not take them seriously. (Remember Herod in 14:3–4?) When the Pharisees test Jesus with the question of divorce, Jesus' response cuts to the core of the problem: divorce was never God's intention for

MAT 6:21

mankind (v. 8) and it was only allowed in special circumstances in the Old Testament because people were so hard hearted (v. 8). Marriage is a whole-life commitment!

When God shows His commitment to us, He uses the picture of marriage (Ephesians 5:25-33). So our relationships in marriage should involve as much commitment as God's relationship with us (and that is a lot of commitment). As we grow, this will mean being very careful in our interactions with members of the opposite sex, otherwise we make marriage look worthless. For some it may mean we never get married – this is not something to be ashamed of. In fact, the apostle Paul speaks about how much of a good thing this can be (1 Corinthians 7:32–35)!

A 'GOOD' MAN COMMITTED TO WEALTH (19:13-26)

Jesus is approached by a man who appears to have it all. He is wealthy (people at the time thought rich people

were favoured by God) and he appears to have kept the Ten Commandments. However, when Jesus asks him to sell his possessions and give to the poor, his actions tell us that his heart actually desires worldly goods and his commitment is to them, not Jesus.

You may think you are not rich, but it doesn't take much for us to become distracted by our possessions. When our hearts our committed to Jesus, we will not fall into this money trap. But a heart that doesn't value the King will seek other 'kings' to follow after.

POOR MEN COMMITTED TO JESUS (19:27-30)

If this rich man, apparently blessed by God, is still not good enough to receive eternal life, how can anyone be saved? Jesus tells us by our efforts alone it's *impossible*! Yikes! But ... with God all things are possible.

It's possible that God can change the hearts of His disciples, who dropped everything they owned and followed Him (v. 27). It's possible that these first servants of the King will one day have places of honour in eternity (v. 28). It's possible that God can change *your* heart to value His will above earthly distractions. With prayer, it is possible that your commitments may change too, and you can look forward to eternal life and the infinite blessing which comes with it (v. 29).

QUESTIONS

- Entertainment, relationships, money, success, popularity, Jesus ... What does your heart truly value?

- How do your actions show this?

A PICTURE OF GRACE

WORKING HARD (20:1-8)

The ancient Jewish work day started at about 6 a.m. – that's right, while you are still drooling all over your pillow! For unemployed people it was extra tough. They would have to wait around in a public area hoping that somebody would give them a job for a day. That's what's happening in this parable.

Can you imagine how you would feel if you worked all day from 6 a.m. only to find out that someone else came onto the jobsite at 5 p.m. and still got paid the same wage as you?

A day's rate for an hour's work! That is so unfair! No wonder the 6 a.m. workers were mad at the employer.

GIVING GOD THE STINK-EYE (20:9-16)

But are we right to be frustrated at this? Why do we get upset? It's because we think rewards should be

MAN WHO HAD NOTHING WAS PAID   MAN WHO HAD NOTHING WAS PAID

measured out by how hard we work. But God doesn't operate like that; *everyone gets what they need.*

You might argue the early worker should get more money because by working longer, he created more value for the landowner. But that forgets two things. Firstly, God can do whatever He wants with His gifts, including not hiring anybody! And secondly, in this story we are not the workers who started early in the morning. Actually, every single one of us is a last-minute chancer who got paid for working one hour!

HARDLY WORKING

The 5 p.m. worker is thankful that the landowner gave what the workers needed, not what they deserved. A day's wage for this poorer part of society was only enough to feed their family for one day, so not getting work could mean a life or death situation for hungry children at home!

50 YEARS OF CHRISTIAN GOOD DEEDS

BEEN A CHRISTIAN FOR FIVE MINUTES!

A REBEL AGAINST GOD WAS OFFERED PEACE

SALVATION

A REBEL AGAINST GOD WAS OFFERED PEACE

GRACE
IS GETTING WHAT WE DON'T DESERVE!

When the landowner hired the late worker, he didn't need an extra hour's work done on the land — he already had plenty of labourers! He looked at the leftover workers with compassion; they needed the money just as much as the early workers. It wasn't fair (as we might think of it) and it wasn't giving each what they deserve, but it pictured the joyful grace of our God.

When we measure our value in the Kingdom, it cannot be done by looking around at other workers. God is not interested in a holiness competition. Instead, we must recognise that we are the needy 5 p.m. worker, and we have an amazing, generous God who gives us forgiveness and peace with Him that we did not earn.

QUESTIONS

- When God gives good things to your friends, how do you respond?
- Are you happy for them or envious?
- Ask God to help you not compare yourself with others around you.

APPROACHING JERUSALEM

NOT AN ACCIDENT (20:17-19)

It's felt like a long journey – and you've only been reading about it! Finally, as Jesus approaches His destination, He reminds

ARE WE NEARLY THERE YET?

JERUSALEM

WELCOME TO GOD'S CITY!

the disciples of what awaits Him. The religious and political authorities will reject Jesus; He will be tortured and then hung on a cross to die. It sounds like a defeat. But despite appearances, none of this is an accident.

Jesus has not only predicted His death three times, but also His resurrection. This bloody defeat at the hands of the Romans will actually be nothing of the sort – Jesus is going to defeat death for all who trust in Him, once and for all. What a victory! God is still very much in charge!

STILL NOT GETTING IT (20:20-28)

Do you know what's awkward? When your Mum asks if you can sit next to God ruling in heaven. However, James and John don't seem too bothered as they back up their Mother's grab for

power. After hearing Jesus talk about humility four times since chapter 18, you would think the lesson might have sunk in: only lowly servants will be called great in God's Kingdom!

These sons of Zebedee *thought* they could be a servant like Jesus was. They *thought* they were strong enough to go the distance and drink the cup of suffering that Jesus was about to drink. But the truth is: all of

...AAAAND ANOTHER THING, JESUS! I WANT YOU TO TEACH MY BOYS HOW TO WALK ON WATER... ALL THESE BOATS AND STORMS... IT'S DANGEROUS! AND WHAT ABOUT ALL THIS STUFF ABOUT SUFFERING?! IF MY BOYS ARE NOT GETTING FED PROPERLY THEN YOU WILL BE HEARING FROM ME! ...SOMEONE TOLD ME MY BOYS HAVE BEEN SLEEPING OUTSIDE! IT'S VERY COLD IN THE EVENINGS AND THEY DON'T HAVE JACKETS ON ...

A MOTHER'S REQUEST (EXTENDED CUT)

Jesus' disciples abandoned Him when things got tough (26:56).

When Jesus was going to the cross, He was the perfect picture of the servant God promised in Isaiah 53:4-6. We should try to be like Him: we are God's servants and should be willing to suffer for His sake. *But* we cannot be like Him in the way James and John wanted.

Only Jesus could suffer for His people as a 'ransom for many'. (We will think more about this later in Matthew.) And only Jesus can be the 'Son of Man' King of Daniel 7:13-14. For this reason, God's people should not try to be superheroes that solve everybody's problems. Rather, we should point others to the only hero they need.

THE BLIND SHALL SEE (20:29-34)

It's ironic that the only individuals who see Jesus clearly as the Son of David – the one who came to save His people – are the two blind men in verses 29–34. The disciples were more concerned about being powerful, but the blind, humble beggars came to Jesus the

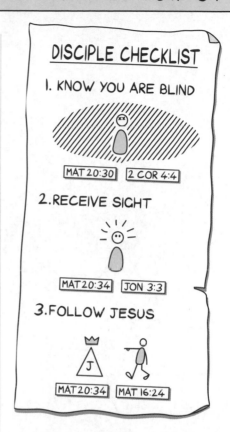

right way (v. 31), and then follow Him faithfully (v. 34).

QUESTIONS

- What are you looking for from Jesus: a ticket to heaven or mercy from the King?

- Pray today for eyes to see Jesus as He truly is, not as you might want Him to be.

THE RETURN OF THE KING

THE KING'S TRIUMPHANT ENTRY (21:1-11)

When Jesus arrives at Jerusalem *everything* kicks off. The crowds following Jesus up until this point have now become huge (v. 8), and when they see Jesus travelling the last couple of miles to Jerusalem by donkey, they don't just see a guy on a donkey, they see God's promised King.

Hundreds of years beforehand, in Zechariah 9:9–11, God promised a King who will come riding on a donkey and set prisoners free. Was *this* that promised King? What would He free

God's people from? In 1 Kings 1:38–40 the first ever 'Son of David' also came riding on a donkey to be made King over Israel. Was *this* Jesus about to be made King over Israel and kick out the Romans? It's not clear how much the crowds outside the gates understood what was going on, but they knew it was going to be epic!

THE LORD RETURNS TO HIS TEMPLE (21:12-17)

However, the crowds inside Jerusalem felt differently; they asked 'Who is this?' (v. 10). Jesus looked like a prophet and a King (v. 11), but

DEATH

the Jerusalem Jews should have seen more. This was God Himself who had arrived – and they should be concerned!

In the last Old Testament book, God gives a final warning to Israel. He promised that one day He would arrive on their doorstep in judgement – suddenly, the Lord would come to His temple. All self-serving religion would be judged (Malachi 3:1–5), but all who approached Him in faith would experience healing (Malachi 4:2).

What a shocker then, when Jesus seemingly arrives out of nowhere one day in Jerusalem, immediately goes to the temple to execute holy justice (vv. 12–13) and while He heals people, children start chanting: 'Son of David!' (vv. 14–15). *And* there was more to come ...

THE FIRST BECOME LAST (21:18-22)

Matthew carefully records the story of the fig tree right between two visits Jesus makes to the temple. God was meant to dwell in this temple; it should be a place of Kingdom care and holiness but it had become an unholy system of money-makers and law-twisters! Horrible! Just like the fig tree, Jesus looked for good fruit from the temple and found none. And just like the fig tree, a serious judgement was coming for the fruitless Jewish leaders. Yikes!

What on earth is going on in this city? Prophecies being fulfilled, crowds going crazy, the sick healed, powerful religious leaders judged ... the Kingdom had come, and everything was being turned upside down.

QUESTIONS

- Do you find the Old Testament boring or confusing?

- Passages like this make it come alive! Why not look up some of the references noted above and see the incredible plan of God?

REFUSING TO REPENT

FROM MAN OR FROM GOD?
(21:23-27)

Beyond the grave, John the Baptist's words were still causing trouble! John announced that Jesus was God's promised King. Now Jesus asks the Pharisees: who gave John permission to say that? If the leaders replied 'from God' then they should have believed what John said about King Jesus, but if they replied 'from man', the crowds would turn against them because they thought John was a God-sent prophet. Since the leaders feared the people rather than God, they dodged the question and refused to recognise Jesus' identity. Awkward!

GO, CLEAN YOUR ROOM

OK

...LIKE A PHARISEE

MAT 21:28-31

HOW TO OBEY...

BETTER LATE THAN NEVER
(21:28-32)

The Jewish leaders were like the second son in Jesus' parable here. On the outside they appear to obey God by praying and following religious rules, but in reality, they don't live God-honouring lives of love and justice like God wants us to. Christians must be like the second son. Even though we may have refused to obey God before now, if we repent and turn to follow Jesus we are welcome in God's Kingdom.

Do you think you have gone too far to be saved? Jesus' point about tax collectors and prostitutes entering the Kingdom tells us two things. Firstly, if we call ourselves a Christian but don't live like it (either publicly or privately) then we are in no better place than people who openly refuse to follow God. However, secondly, if we think we have lived a life so bad that we have crossed a line of no return; we are wrong. Whatever you have done in the past, you are *never* too bad to make a fresh start with God.

JESUS WAS REJECTED BY THE OLD TESTAMENT PEOPLE OF GOD

GET LOST!

JESUS IS NOW THE CORNERSTONE OF THE NEW COVENANT PEOPLE OF GOD (THE CHURCH)

EPH 2:20

PROFITS AND PROPHETS (21:33-46)

We know this because throughout history God has repeatedly come to His people looking to forgive those who repent, just like the parable of the tenants explains. The servants of the vineyard owner repeatedly came to seek the owner's fair share of the income from the vineyard. In the same way, God has repeatedly sent prophets to the Jewish religious leaders that they may give Him what He is owed – lives that honour Him.

But God doesn't get this. When the son is sent in the parable, the tenants reject him and kill him. In turn, the owner will destroy the tenants and give his vineyard to those who will produce fruit for him (v. 43). Such grace! Despite these rascals, God is still seeking tenants for His vineyard! Are you willing to give Him the fruit He is owed?

QUESTIONS

- The Jewish leaders cared more about the opinion of others than the opinion of God. Where does this lead them?

- How is your behaviour affected by the opinion of friends or family?

75

THE KING HAS INVITED YOU!

THE GOSPEL OF THE KING (22:1-7)

The Kingdom of Heaven is like a wedding banquet! If you like good food and parties (and let's face it, who doesn't) then *why* would you ever reject God's invitation to celebrate?

Well, if you're like the Jewish leaders, you might have rejected God's invitation because you're busy doing your own thing (v. 5). Or, you might reject God because you don't like God's rules. Or perhaps you are holding something against Him; it might be that you hate God (v. 6). Perhaps this is you; perhaps this is your friends?

Whatever the case, God's invitation is open today. Think about what celebrating with the God of the universe would be like! Think about the clinking glasses, tasty food and partying with God's massive family! And by the way, did you notice it's free entry (v. 4)? Now *that's* my kind of party.

MODERN DAY MESSENGERS (22:8-10)

In this parable, Christians are not only the 'bad and the good' people who are later invited to the wedding (v. 10), but we are also the servants of God handing out invites. When we tell other people about the King's message, it should not feel like a list of dos and don'ts, but like an invitation to the only party worth going to.

DISHONOURING THE KING (22:11-14)

It's a big deal being invited to a royal wedding, that's why people arrive wearing ridiculous hats. Only your fanciest clothes are appropriate to show respect for such a privilege. But what about if the King of the universe calls you to His Son's wedding? Surely your whole life would have to reflect what an honour that is, never mind your clothes!

So when 'scruffy Joe' in verse 11, turns up in Jeans and a t-shirt, his lack of respect dishonours the King who has already been so gracious to him. As a result, he is cast out. If we think we can come to God saying 'I am a Christian responding to your invitation' and then later, God finds that we have not changed our lives to honour the King, then we will be in the same position.

Verse 14 is a reminder: only those who have been *chosen* are given 'ears to hear' Jesus' words (13:9) and live like the King wants. How can we know if we are chosen? Simple: anyone who responds humbly to God's invitation, even today, has already been chosen by God.

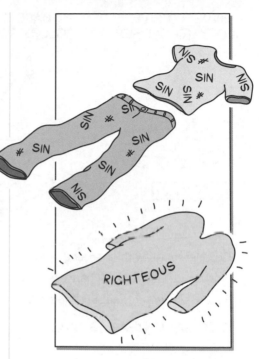

WE GET OUR WEDDING CLOTHES FROM GOD
ISAIAH 61:10

QUESTIONS

- This parable shows God as a generous King and highest judge. One picture may make us joyful, the other scared. Out of these two ways, how are you more likely to think of God?

- How can you remember that God is both loving and holy?

UNCERTAINTY OF DEATH AND TAXES

MADE TO GIVE
GLORY TO CAESER

MAT 22:21

MADE TO GIVE
GLORY TO CAESER

MADE TO GIVE
GLORY TO GOD

GEN 1:26-27

Getting smart with a teacher never works out well – the Pharisees and Sadducees find this out in chapter 22.

GIVE BACK WHAT IS OWED (22:15–22)

The Pharisees first try to trick Jesus with this question: 'should we pay taxes to an anti-Jewish government?' If Jesus said 'yes' then the Jewish people would turn on Him. If Jesus said 'no' the Romans would very quickly jail Him as a rebel. Sneaky!

However, Jesus manages to answer without falling into their trap. He asks for a Roman coin to demonstrate.

Caesar's image was on the coin and it was Caesar's Roman government that spent the tax money so all Roman coins and taxes belonged to Caesar. If Roman money belonged to Caesar, then it's fair for Caesar to ask for some of it back (today Christians should pay our taxes for the same reason). However, the question is: what belongs to God (v. 21)?

Everything; and the Pharisees knew it (Psalm 24:1)! We are stamped with God's image (Genesis 1:26–28), we breathe God's air, and we eat God's food! So, if everything belongs to God, then how much do we owe God? Everything.

GOD IS GOD (22:23–33)

The next question was from the Sadducees. Unlike Jesus, they believed death was the final full stop in life; when people died, that was it. To them, death was so powerful that it stops everything, including marriage. They were partially right. Jesus explains that human marriage only lasts as long as both the married people are alive on earth; nobody remains married in heaven.

But they are wrong about death being the end – in God's Kingdom this is far from true!

Jesus reminds them of God's full title: 'I am the God of Abraham, Isaac and Jacob' (see Exodus 3:6). The Sadducees had failed to notice that this means God is *still* the God of these three men who had died. (God's name is *'I am'* not 'I was'!) If God is the God 'of the living' (v. 32), and God is the God of these three men who died, then these three men must *still* be living somehow – God raises people from the dead!

In other words, not even death could stop the Lord's promise to be God to these men – God is far too alive for that. Death *was*. But God *is*! If God is *still* God to dead men (meaning they are actually still alive) then surely you who live today can trust God all the way to the grave and beyond.

HOW OFTEN ARE WE IN ERROR...

...BECAUSE WE DO NOT KNOW THE SCRIPTURES...

J

...OR THE POWER OF GOD?

MAT 22:29

QUESTIONS

Don't just skim over the idea of living forever. Imagine physically living in a New Creation with God. Take time to praise Him for making this possible through Jesus.

THE BIG QS!

THE GREATEST COMMANDMENT(S) (22:34-40)

Have you ever asked a simple question and got a more complicated answer? So annoying! However, it usually means you didn't ask the right question!

When the Pharisees come back at Jesus with another attack, they ask Him what *one* commandment sums up the 600+ rules of the Old Testament. But Jesus gives *two* answers; love God and love others. Why do we need both answers?

Think of Christian living like flying in a helicopter. Just like a helicopter needs a main rotor and a tail rotor to take off, a Christian needs to love God and love others to obey Jesus. We can try and just love God, without ever gathering with His people or caring for them, and that might look very impressive for a moment. But as we take off, if we do not love people as God loves them (so much that He died for them!) then like a helicopter without a tail rotor, we will spin around and crash. On the other hand, if we try and love others without first loving God, then we will never take off

'I ONLY LOVE GOD, NOT PEOPLE!'

'I ONLY LOVE PEOPLE, NOT GOD!'

'I LOVE GOD AND LOVE PEOPLE AS GOD WANTS ME TO'

at all. Only with both rotors spinning can we live as Jesus commanded!

THE LORD SAID TO MY LORD (22:41-45)

Has your Mum or Dad ever called you 'Boss'? Didn't think so. *They* are the boss of *you*! Jesus puts a similar question to the Pharisees: how can we explain what King David said in the Old Testament?

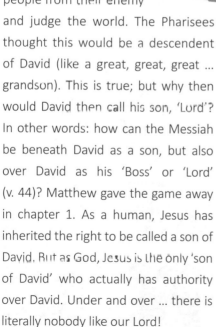

In Psalm 110, King David speaks about the promised Messiah who will save God's people from their enemy and judge the world. The Pharisees thought this would be a descendent of David (like a great, great, great ... grandson). This is true; but why then would David then call his son, 'Lord'? In other words: how can the Messiah be beneath David as a son, but also over David as his 'Boss' or 'Lord' (v. 44)? Matthew gave the game away in chapter 1. As a human, Jesus has inherited the right to be called a son of David. But as God, Jesus is the only 'son of David' who actually has authority over David. Under and over ... there is literally nobody like our Lord!

SATISFIED? (22:46)

Well, that shut them up! The Pharisees were amazed (v. 22), the crowds were astonished (v. 33) and nobody dared to ask more questions (v. 46). You won't find this kind of wisdom from normal people in the world. We should be amazed too – this wisdom comes from God!

WORDS AREN'T WORKING! ...ON TO PLAN B

QUESTIONS

How can you show love for God and others when you are at school?

What about at home, on the football pitch, in a music lesson or on holiday?

A PICTURE OF BAD RELIGION

BAD RELIGION THINKS ITSELF GREATER THAN OTHERS (23:1–12)

If you have ever accidently called a teacher 'Mum', then you know that titles matter. Different titles show who is in charge (who has authority). For example, the Jews here were teachers called *'rabbis'* (no ... 'rabbis' not 'rabbits'!). And Jesus taught that they should be obeyed in the same way Israel's first great teacher was obeyed (vv. 2–3).

PHARISAIC LEADERSHIP

But the problem was they loved this authority! They *loved* looking important and making people follow them. They would even make others obey rules that they themselves could not keep! God put them in charge to help the people, but they used that authority to make others feel small.

Christian leaders are instead meant to be servants. Our leaders should not love great titles like 'father' or 'instructor' (vv. 9–10). Instead, God's word (the Bible) must always be the Christian's highest authority. Usually we can trust our Christian leaders, but if a teacher says something that disagrees with the Bible, go with the Bible!

BAD RELIGION THINKS LOOKING GOOD IS REALLY IMPORTANT (23:13–36)

Imagine you are thirsty and someone offers you two cans of juice. The first can is unopened, but has fallen in some dirt. The second can is clean and beautifully polished, but when you

look inside, it is filled with maggots. Which would you choose to drink?

That is something like how God sees bad religion. It may look good on the outside, but inside it is disgusting. We can go to church, smile at people and even hold the door open every now and then ... but if we do these things just to look good but we don't really live like that the rest of the time, then we are no better than the Pharisees. Just like the second can needs to be rinsed out and filled with something good, we need our sins forgiven and to be filled with the Holy Spirit.

BAD RELIGION IS CARED FOR BUT JUDGED (23.37-39)

Time and time again God came to the Jewish leaders, longing to care for them as closely and warmly as a hen cares for her chicks (v. 37). Even though the bad religion of the Pharisees was disgusting to God, He was still calling them to gather under His protective wings. It was too late for these leaders,

who are about to be thrown away like a rotten can of juice, but for those reading this today, it's not too late to chuck out the bad religion in our lives.

QUESTIONS

○ Do you do some things so that others think you are a 'good Christian'?

○ Instead of making yourself look good, what does Jesus want you to do (v. 11)?

GOD HAS LEFT THE TEMPLE

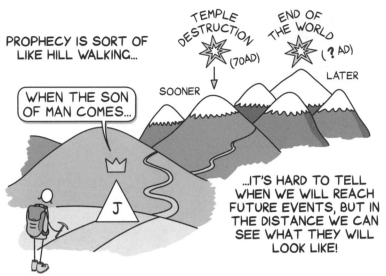

PROPHECY IS SORT OF LIKE HILL WALKING...

TEMPLE DESTRUCTION (70AD)

END OF THE WORLD (? AD)

LATER

SOONER

WHEN THE SON OF MAN COMES...

J

...IT'S HARD TO TELL WHEN WE WILL REACH FUTURE EVENTS, BUT IN THE DISTANCE WE CAN SEE WHAT THEY WILL LOOK LIKE!

So what was all *that* scary stuff about? Matthew 24 is filled with prophecy about end times — the end of the temple and the end of the world. Even today Christians are still debating the details of what Jesus said here, but there are some things we can be really sure of …

THE TEMPLE WILL BE DESTROYED

When Jesus leaves the temple (v. 1), He isn't just going for some fresh air, He is leaving it forever! As we see in the Old Testament, God has repeatedly asked Israel to turn from their sin to follow Him properly. Now, Jesus has given the Jewish leaders their last chance. When they finally reject Jesus, He promises to come back to the temple again, but this time in judgement.

We know the frightening things Jesus speaks of here actually happened in A.D. 70 when the Romans destroyed the Jewish temple, 40 years after Jesus predicting it. This horrible attack was God's judgement on the Jews, but for the Romans it was a great victory. In fact, they made a stone carving celebrating this event — you can still see it in Rome today.

But as we will discover in tomorrow's section: the destruction of the temple also helps us know what it will be like when Jesus returns one day to judge the *whole earth*. For the Jews, their entire lives revolved around this one temple, so when it was destroyed in A.D. 70 it must have felt like the end of the world! Today we must learn their lesson. When King Jesus returns, those in His Kingdom will be safe. But for those who refuse Him, everything will be destroyed.

HARDSHIPS WILL COME

In the run up to the temple destruction, Christians were being put to death, people were doing evil things and, as historians from the time tell us, the Roman Emperor was seen as a (false) Messiah figure. These events were meant to warn the disciples: Jesus was about to destroy the temple. When we see similar hardships today, we should be reminded that Jesus is coming back soon to judge and to save.

YOU CAN READ ABOUT THE DESTRUCTION OF THE TEMPLE FROM ANCIENT HISTORIANS...

'HISTORIES' TACITUS (BOOK 5)

'THE JEWISH WAR' FLAVIUS JOSEPHUS

...SEARCH FOR IT ONLINE!

JESUS' DISCIPLES MUST HANG ON TO THE KING

In the midst of all this, Jesus doesn't want His disciples to be afraid. Because:

FACTS

- JESUS WILL SAVE THOSE WHO STAND FIRM IN HARDSHIPS. (24:13)

- THE KINGDOM MESSAGE MUST STILL BE PREACHED TO THE WORLD. (24:14)

- WHEN THE KING COMES BACK, YOU WON'T MISS IT. (24:27)

- UNLIKE EVERYTHING ELSE IN LIFE, JESUS AND HIS WORDS WILL NEVER FAIL YOU, BETRAY YOU, OR PASS AWAY. (24:35)

If we are Christians, we have nothing to fear from the end of the world. In fact, Jesus' return means a final end to all the pain and suffering of a broken planet; definitely something worth praying for.

QUESTIONS

If Jesus can predict all these events, how much do you think God knows about your future? Why does this matter?

THE KING IS COMING!

WHEN WILL THE END COME? (24:36)

'None of your business!' is one answer to that question!

Despite Jesus clearly saying that *'only the Father'* knows the day of the Son's return (24:36), many groups have made predictions about when

A JOYLESS AND DANGEROUS WAY TO LIVE →

Jesus will come back. Sometimes people will even give up their whole lives thinking that there will be no tomorrow! But Christians shouldn't play dangerous guessing games like this: when the end comes, we will be doing normal, everyday things like everybody else (24:40–41).

A SUDDEN SEPARATION (24:37–41)

Jesus does not tell us a specific day that He will return, but He is *very* specific about one thing: when He comes back, there will be no chance to react, even to repent. For those who have been ignoring or refusing Jesus' call, they are separated off and there is no opportunity to realise their terrible mistake. (That's why it's important to speak to people about Jesus now, not later.) But at the same time, for those who are part of His Kingdom, the moment the King gathers us in will be wonderful. It means we will never have to truly say goodbye to one another (24:31; 25:10).

GUARDS, SERVANTS, BRIDESMAIDS (24:42–25:13)

What do these three people have in common? They are all waiting for something!

Christians are to be guards. Nobody expects a thief to break in, and nobody expects Jesus to return – except guards! We must be alert to Jesus' return.

Christians are to be good servants. We have been put in charge of the important job of living out and speaking God's message to the world. However, don't slack off just because Jesus hasn't returned for 2000 years ... Instead, imagine if Jesus came back to find you praying, and living a life guided by His word — what an honour awaits (24:47)!

Finally, Christians are to be wise bridesmaids. (No, that doesn't mean you get to wear a pretty

OIL IN HERE

dress.) In ancient Jewish culture, bridesmaids would wait for the groom to arrive at the wedding party. Those with lit torches were identified as the real bridesmaids (not party crashers) and so they were allowed in. But any bridesmaid without a lit torch would be treated as a stranger in the darkness. Today, there may be many people who say they are a Christian because of one reason or another, but only those lit up with faith in Jesus will be allowed into the wonderful wedding feast. Don't miss out — be prepared!

QUESTIONS

Will all my friends be saved? When will this happen? Will I be around for this event? Some things we are not meant to know. Give these questions over to God and ask for help in living the simple daily life of the Kingdom.

HOW THE KING DECIDES

Are you a good enough person to be given eternal life by King Jesus (v. 46)? If we don't listen to Jesus' words in chapter 25, we will worry about this question forever.

GOD HAS MADE AN INVESTMENT (25:14-30)

When we become a Christian, God gives us His Holy Spirit. God Himself lives in us. That alone is a gift worth far more than a lifetime supply of gold! If this is true, what would be worse: hiding a gift of money in the ground (like the bad servant) or hiding God's gift of the Spirit? God blesses us so that we can bless others! If we are only a Christian to 'get to heaven' and we don't live like Kingdom people, we are behaving like the bad servant (vv. 24–25).

Two bags of gold, five bags of gold … the master gives to each servant 'according to his ability' (v. 15) and each good servant was hugely rewarded (vv. 21, 23). Not every Christian gets the same gifts but every Christian who uses what they have gets a reward!

THE SHEEP ARE SAVED (25:31-33)

Hold on there, eager beaver! Before we rush off and try and earn our way into God's Kingdom, let's hear more about Jesus' final decision.

In verses 31–33, we see that the Son of Man will be like a shepherd, splitting up a flock into two groups of animals: sheep and goats. The sheep will be with God forever, the goats will be rejected by God forever. Jesus'

THERE IS ALWAYS SOMEONE MORE GIFTED THAN YOU!

BUT HOW ARE YOU USING THE GIFTS YOU HAVE?

final decision, the most important decision in the world, is *not* based on how much of a difference we have made in God's Kingdom. It's based on whether we are a sheep or a goat, whether we follow Jesus as our shepherd or not.

THE SAVED ARE GOOD (25:34-46)

But wait a minute there, super sheep! Not everyone who calls Jesus 'Lord, Lord' will be saved (remember 7:21?) and not everyone who bleats like a farm animal is really a sheep! It's what you *do* that shows who you *are*.

God's people care for others in need (v. 40). Just like apples only come from apple trees, loving others as Jesus loved us can only come from being a 'Christian tree' (remember 7:18–20?). Again, it's what you *do* that shows who you *are*.

Let's answer the question at the start; you will *never ever* be good enough to be given eternal life by King Jesus. (Yikes!) *But* if you live with Jesus as your King, then you don't need to be good enough – you

MIXING UP JESUS' PARABLES GETS CONFUSING

may be a sinful sheep, but you have eternal life in His fold.

QUESTIONS

How can you use your talents, gifts or personality to serve Jesus and His church?

JESUS BETRAYED

PASSOVER PREPARATIONS (26:1–5)

Think about when God saved His people from slavery in Egypt. Because of Pharaoh's hard heart, God sent ten plagues on the land – the last of these was death (Exodus 12:1–30). All the firstborn sons of the land were to die. However, God's people could paint the blood of a lamb onto the doorframe of their house, and instead of taking any life inside, the Lord would 'pass over' that house. Instead of the firstborn son dying, a lamb died in his place.

When Pharaoh refused to release God's people from slavery, his son and many others died in Egypt. But, because God's people trusted in Him and sacrificed a lamb, the faithful Israelite families were safe.

In Jesus' time, Passover was a big festival to celebrate God's rescue that day. But the people had no idea there was about to be another lamb sacrificed. This lamb's blood, the blood of Jesus, wouldn't just save one household; this sacrifice would save all God's people, forever!

BURIAL BEGINNINGS (26:6–13)

The disciples cried 'what a waste!' as a woman poured expensive perfume on Jesus' head. But Jesus tells them off; whether she knew it or not, this woman was lovingly preparing Jesus' body to be buried. He was going to die.

Would His body get covered with sweat and blood later? Yes. Does that mean her perfuming efforts were wasted? No way. Whatever we do out of love for Jesus, whether a big

or little thing, success or failure, it's never a waste. This woman is still remembered today for such love.

DECEPTION DECIDED (26:14-16)

Matthew told us about Judas in chapter 10, but it's still shocking to see him betray Jesus. The Jewish leaders wanted Jesus dead, but they needed to get Him away from the crowds to avoid a riot (v. 46). So in secret, they paid for an inside man: Judas, the betrayer.

Jesus promises everything for those in His Kingdom – even eternal life. But Judas threw it all away for some coins! What a painful trade! What a dark deed! It's true: 'the love of money is a root of all kinds of evil' (1 Timothy 6:10).

EVERYTHING PLANNED (26:17-25)

Have you noticed, Jesus knew He was going to be betrayed by Judas, crucified and buried. God worked all this together at this precise time so that Jesus could be the Passover lamb for us. None of this was an accident! Even when things look horrible, God is in control.

QUESTIONS

If you trust in Him, Jesus' sacrifice rescues you from slavery too. What slavery does He rescue you from? (Paul helps explain in Romans 6:15-23. It's tricky to read, but give it a go!)

THE LAST SUPPER

EATING FLESH? (26:26)

When the disciples ate the broken bread, it was a picture of Jesus' death. Just as the bread was broken, Jesus' body was going to be broken. But also, by telling the disciples to eat this broken bread, He was picturing how important His death would be for those who follow Him. We need to eat bread to stay physically alive – we need to 'eat' (trust in) Jesus' death to be spiritually alive!

DRINKING BLOOD? (26:27-30)

The wine was a picture of Jesus' blood. But what's so important about blood? Well, to understand the blood, we have to understand sin.

Sin and God don't mix – *ever*. If we have ever sinned, we can never be with God unless our sin is dealt with. This needs more than just an apology – the punishment for sin and the cost of sin is death (Romans 6:23)!

But God had a plan – if there was a death, if there was a blood payment, sin could be put away and the people could still be part of God's family. So God made a special arrangement (called a *covenant*) which allowed His people to provide blood through the death of animals and promises to obey God rather than keep on sinning (check out Exodus 24:7–8). But, God's people were still disobedient, and no matter how many animals were sacrificed, their blood was never enough to pay for sin … a special sacrifice was needed.

When Jesus tells the disciples that *His* blood is the 'blood of the covenant' (v. 28), we know *He* will be the one who pays the punishment of death that we deserve for our sins. He has never sinned and His sacrifice is worth way more than the blood of animals. Anyone who 'drinks' Jesus' blood (trusts in Him) is forever forgiven for their sins!

MAKING PROMISES (26:31-35)

After this meal, Jesus reads an Old Testament prophecy which predicts what's about to happen – Jesus will be struck down and His disciples will run away. Simon Peter can't believe his ears and makes a foolhardy promise: 'Even if everyone else leaves and I have to die, I will never leave your side!'

But even this leading disciple is unable to save Jesus, himself or anybody! He talks big, but his promises mean nothing (v. 34). However, Jesus knows exactly what's about to happen, and the covenant promises He made will never be broken. In life we can either rely on human strength or the promises of God – which are you putting your trust in?

JESUS' BLOOD IS SPILLED - NOT YOURS

A SURE PROMISE

OF SALVATION...

JESUS' BODY IS BROKEN - NOT YOURS

TO ALL

WHO BELIEVE

QUESTIONS

- How do you feel about 'communion' or 'the Lord's supper' at church?
- What does it mean to some of the older Christians you know? Ask them!

ALL BY GOD'S WILL

OBEYING THE FATHER (26:36-46)

If you are a naughty kid (yes, you, reading this book!) you might know how it feels to wait outside the head teacher's office before getting told off. Or maybe you have heard the words 'just wait until your Father gets home!' That time of waiting before being punished is almost as bad as the punishment itself!

Imagine then, how Jesus feels waiting to receive a terrible punishment that He doesn't deserve – in a few hours He will drink from the cup of God's wrath that *we* deserve! It's not like the cup the disciples drank in verse 27. *This* cup is filled with God's anger towards our sin and rebellion against God's Kingdom. When Jesus

drinks from this cup, He saves us from the worst thing you could ever think of (check out Jeremiah 25:30–31).

Even though Jesus is terrified and prays for any other way He could save His people, there is none. He loves the Father and so obeys Him until the end (v. 42). He loves *you* so much that Jesus faces hell so you don't have to.

KISS OF DEATH (26:47-49)

Being betrayed is never nice, especially by a close friend. Yet, even at His lowest moment so far, Jesus must now face the betrayal of a disciple (as He prophesied in 20:18; 26:2; 26:20–25). In the quiet of this night-time garden, Judas takes the opportunity to help the Jewish leaders capture Jesus in secret. When they arrive, Judas personally greets his teacher to show the mob who they should grab in the darkness.

NOT BY THE SWORD (26:50-56)

Throughout all this, the disciples have been worse than useless. When Jesus wanted the comfort and prayers of friends earlier, they were asleep. Now, after Jesus has willingly given Himself up, one of them is flailing a sword about trying to protect the King of the universe! (This is sort of like trying to protect a lion from being attacked by a hamster – the lion can handle it.)

Jesus doesn't need mighty warriors for His Kingdom – at any point He could call down 60,000 angels to

in the darkest moments (and there are no moments darker than what we are about to read) God is always in charge.

defend Him (v. 53)! Moreover, Jesus knows that people who use violence to get their way will have their ways ended by violence (v. 52). No, unlike the panicking disciples, Jesus remembers that these events are all part of the plan (vv. 54, 56). Even

QUESTIONS

- Is Jesus being forced to take our punishment (John 10:17-18)?

- How does this passage tell us trusting in Jesus is the only way we can be right with God (v. 39)?

A JEWISH JUDGEMENT

GOD JUDGED BY HIS OWN PEOPLE (26:57–68)

The Jewish leaders aren't allowed to just kill Jesus on the spot. But if they could prove He was a serious criminal, they could bring Him to the Romans for 'legal' execution. Of course, there is nothing legal about any of the courts Jesus is brought before. Everything is hushed and rushed (as bad deeds often are) and a Jewish court is set up in the middle of the night to try and find people who would accuse Jesus of a crime. Even the testimony about Jesus destroying the temple is not actually what Jesus said (see Matthew 24:1–2), but the High Priest doesn't really care.

Caiaphas was more interested in Jesus' identity. If he could get Jesus to say that He was the Messiah, the Son of God, he could accuse Jesus of making Himself a Jewish King (which the Romans would punish with death) or accuse Jesus of making Himself equal to God (which was blasphemy, also punishable by death).

When Jesus answers, He not only suggests Caiaphas is correct, but He again brings up the picture of Daniel 7:13–14, where the Son of Man comes on the clouds of heaven and is given all Kingdoms to rule over. They think that Jesus is in the docks being judged, but in reality, they are about to be judged by Jesus, the Son of Man, in the courtroom of God! As you can imagine, such a suggestion did not go down well with the High Priest and Jesus is sent off to the Romans to have His fate decided.

GODLY SORROW AND WORLDLY REGRET (26:69–27:10)

While this is going on, Simon Peter is also on trial. As Jesus prophesied, Peter denies any involvement with

CAIAPHAS

HIGH PRIEST AD 18–36

RELIGION: JEWISH

SPEAKS TO JESUS: IN HIS PALACE

SPHERE OF POWER: RELIGIOUS

ATTACK: ACCUSES JESUS OF BLASPHEMY

his friend. Peter is right to be deeply upset as a result; he might be remembering Jesus' serious words earlier in 10:33. However, even this sin can be forgiven and we can read about how Peter is once again made right with God in John 21:15–19.

Judas was sorry in a different way. He felt guilty for betraying an innocent man, and the money he made from his evil act was of no help. But, Judas' sin was no brief mistake. It was a careful plan to destroy God's King. At no point, not even in the last moments of life, did Judas seek forgiveness from God. Peter turned away from denying Jesus ever again;

Judas only wanted to stop feeling guilty. When we sin, we must be sorry like Peter and not like Judas.

THINKING ABOUT SUICIDE

Humans are made in the Image of God (Genesis 1:27). This means you have value – you are very important to Him! Trying to kill a person made in God's image (either yourself or someone else) is therefore very serious in God's eyes. There may be times where we feel like suicide is a good way out from the pain of life, but it never is.

PSALM 51

A PICTURE OF REPENTANCE

– WHY NOT USE THE WORDS OF THIS PSALM TO HELP YOU LEARN HOW TO REPENT?

REMEMBER

Jesus' suffering in these passages means He knows what we are going through (Hebrews 4:15). Even people who wrote the Bible felt such darkness, but with God, pain never wins the day. (The Psalmists often felt like this. Have a look at Psalms 23 and 42.)

A ROMAN RULING

JUST ONE CONCERN (27:11-14)

People often have lots to say about Jesus, and often it's noisy nonsense! It was the same when Jesus walked the earth. There were accusations firing at Him left, right and centre, but Jesus gave no response to the Roman governor. This man, Pilate, will decide Jesus' fate. Why doesn't Jesus defend Himself?

It's because nonsense accusations did not matter. Just like in the Jewish court, Jesus only answers questions about His identity. The big question of Matthew has not changed: 'who do you say that I am?' (16:15).

The Jewish leaders said Jesus was a liar and blasphemer; but who do you say that He is? Pilate was only concerned to find out if Jesus was an enemy King looking to cause trouble for Rome; but who do you say that He is? That's the big question for us all!

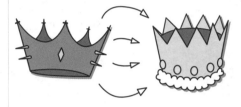

THE ENEMY APPROACHES (27:15-20)

If Judas only wanted money, Pilate only wanted power. He saw Jesus wasn't a threat, so in a bid to gain some political points he organises a big display at the Passover festival. Early that morning, the Jerusalem crowd gathered nearby and were allowed to choose between two prisoners. The prisoner they chose would be released.

The leaders stirred up the crowd and they choose the criminal Barabbas to go free. Even worse, they want the innocent Jesus brutally killed. They cry out, let 'His blood be on us and on our children!' (v. 25). Where has this

PUNISHED AND DIDN'T DESERVE IT — SET FREE AND DIDN'T DESERVE IT

outrageous evil come from? In the battle between Kingdoms, is Satan about to have his way (12:22–28)?

A TRADE IS MADE (27:21-31)

Nobody really thought Jesus was guilty. Pilate washed his hands in an attempt to remove his part in the events, his wife had a dream telling her Jesus was innocent, and it was obvious the Jewish leaders were only accusing Him out of self-interest (v. 18). Yet Jesus was sent to be crucified.

Barabbas, however, was a rebel and a murderer (Mark 15:7). In contrast to Jesus, *nobody* thought he was innocent! And yet – this man walked free.

When we look at the cross in the next few passages, we are not innocent bystanders. Matthew puts us in the story ... in the place of Barabbas! We too were rebels against God's Kingdom, waiting to be punished. But Jesus takes the rebel's punishment that we deserve. What a trade! We are guilty, but we go free!

QUESTIONS

- How would you feel if someone took your place in prison?

- If you trust in Jesus, this is a small picture of what has really happened to you. Take some time today to tell God how you feel about this.

'HERE'S YOUR KING!'

From the start, Jesus spoke about God's coming Kingdom (4:17). Perhaps the soldiers remembered this as they mocked Him in a pretend coronation ceremony. They have no idea that their mocking is really an ugly picture of what is about to happen – Jesus will soon be seated on a heavenly throne.

THE KING IS CROWNED (27:27-30)

One day, every knee will bow before King Jesus, but for now, it's done in cruel jest. How ridiculous! These soldiers attack Jesus and dress Him in an old Roman robe; but soon He will wear the royal robe of a King victorious in battle over His enemies (Revelation 19:13). They thrust a painful crown of thorns onto His head, but soon this King will wear crowns upon crowns (Revelation 19:12)! The soldiers get a stick and pretend it is a Kingly sceptre, but Jesus' sceptre of rule will be as hard as iron (Revelation 19:15). They call Him the 'King of the Jews', but He is much more than this; Jesus is soon to be crowned 'King of all Kings' (Revelation 19:16). So why is Jesus taking all this?

THE KING'S WALK (27:31-33)

Jesus suffers because His Kingdom requires it. Remember when

Jesus prophesied His crucifixion in Matthew 16:24–28? Simon Peter wanted to stop it from happening, but Jesus reminded him that God's Kingdom people must 'take up their cross' – just like their King. Not that's exactly what we see. A different Simon gives us a picture of what being a disciple looks like: carrying the cross given to us for the sake of our King.

THE KING IS ON HIS THRONE (27:34-44)

While Jesus was on the cross between two rebels, everyone now joins in the mocking. What they shout at Jesus may look familiar: *'if you are the Son of God … save yourself!'* This same phrase came from the mouth of Satan at the start of Jesus' ministry (4:3, 4.6); now His Kingly mission ends with the same devilish shout.

So why *did* God choose to die on a cross? Some find the idea too messy for today's neat and tidy religion. Others think the idea is nuts! For many more people, the idea that Jesus died to deal with our sins is simply too offensive. But to those in God's Kingdom, this is the central point of history, our only way

to know the Father. That man on the cross is our King, and He is about to defeat our worst enemy forever.

QUESTIONS

Read Psalm 22:1-21. It was written hundreds of years before these events, but can you see what it is describing?

JESUS DIED: SO WHAT?

JESUS DRINKS GOD'S WRATH (27:45-50)

If you were outside at midday and everything suddenly went dark, you might get a bit freaked out. However, if you were standing in front of the Son of God at Passover time, and then it went dark ... you might think the end was coming!

The Jews nearby would know that at the first Passover, thousands of years ago, God showed His anger against Pharaoh by sending ten plagues. The ninth plague was a darkness that covered the whole land ... the tenth plague was the death of the firstborn son (we looked at this on Day 41).

Under this new plague of darkness, God was again showing His anger. This time, it was directed at His *own* Son – the Son of God. Jesus was now drinking the cup of wrath that *we* deserve because of our sin. For a time, Jesus' close relationship with the Father is broken and there's no prophet Elijah coming to save Him (27:49) – Jesus really is alone as He takes the sin of the world on His own shoulders.

THE WAY TO GOD IS NOW OPEN (27:51-53)

When Jesus died, the punishment for sin was completely and fully paid. No wonder the world around rippled with God's power!

Firstly, we see the temple curtain tear from top to bottom – certainly not by a human hand! This curtain once separated a sinful people from their sinless God. But now, Jesus has destroyed this barrier and opened up the way to the Lord for anyone who has their sins paid for by Jesus' death.

Secondly, God also caused an earthquake which split open tombs! Dead bodies sprang to life! Jesus had not only defeated sin, but the worst effect of sin — death! God raised these people with real, physical bodies for all to see. Have you

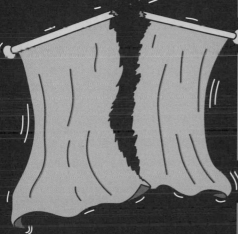

been as well respected as men at the time) showed great courage and were still faithfully watching. Even more incredibly, the most barbaric, violent soldiers who tortured Jesus only hours before now see what's going on and exclaim — 'this really was the Son of God!'

put your trust in Jesus? If so such a moment awaits you too. One day all of Jesus' followers will be raised with a wonderful, real, resurrection body.

ANYONE CAN BELIEVE (27:54-66)

Once again, the unexpected becomes expected in Jesus' Kingdom. The 'brave' disciples had run off ... but the women (who would not have

QUESTIONS

Here's what to remember from this passage: God's wrath against sin is put on Jesus, the payment of death for sin is paid by Jesus, and the way to God is open for anyone because of Jesus! Do you feel secure in Him?

JESUS IS ALIVE

THE SUPERNATURAL AND THE NATURAL (28:1-7)

If you have ever lost someone you love, you know that graveyards feel like very quiet, final places. The dirt is still, the grass grows slowly and the gravestones are cold and hard … but not this day.

This day, when the two faithful Marys go to Jesus' tomb (which would be more like a cave, above ground) they find nothing but *life*. With a shake of the earth, an angel of the Lord appears and shifts the huge stone that was blocking the tomb entrance. The angel's clothes are intensely white,

and the guards are so terrified that they become the most dead-looking thing in the cemetery (v. 4)!

So now Jesus has a chance to escape, right? Nope – He's already gone! This supernatural angel provides the most natural of proof: there's no body (v. 6)! Just like with these women, God never asks us for 'blind faith', there is always evidence to look at.

SEE JESUS, WILL WORSHIP (28:8-10)

Sometimes when you see something spectacular, you simply have to marvel. The Scottish Highlands are breath-taking. Angels are (apparently) terrifying. But at the sight of Jesus Christ who has once and for all defeated death for you and for me … people fall down in *worship*.

Only days ago, *this* Jesus was hanging dead from a wooden cross – now He stands in the flesh saying 'Hello!' Awe and wonder simply doesn't cut the mustard! The only reaction that makes sense for these two women is to fall down in humble worship at the feet of the Lord Almighty.

'YOU HAD ONE JOB!' (28:11-15)

The whole point of putting a guard in front of the tomb was to stop Jesus' body going anywhere (27:62–66). But now these soldiers had to tell

OK - HERE'S WHAT WE WILL SAY...

A GROUP OF DISCIPLES...

(YES, THE ONES WHO RAN AWAY THE OTHER NIGHT)

...THEY CAME IN THE NIGHT WHILE YOU (TRAINED GUARDS) WERE **ASLEEP**...

Z z z

...AND THEY STOLE THE BODY TO MAKE PEOPLE THINK JESUS WAS THE MESSIAH!

HEH HEH

the Jewish leaders that nothing could stop Jesus rising from the dead — not a huge stone at the entrance or their strongest armed forces!

After looking, even the chief priests had to admit the body was gone! But because they wanted to hang onto power, and because the soldiers were more interested in money, they all pretended that a small group of untrained disciples stole the body from armed military men.

Today, we have so much evidence showing Jesus really did rise from the grave, but don't take my word for it, look it up! What could be more important than being sure about this fact? Jesus really died. He really did rise from the dead. And He really did do all this for you.

BUT IF JESUS IS STILL DEAD... WHY WOULD THEY RISK THEIR LIVES FOR A LIE?

OI! OH NO

OH I DON'T KNOW! THEY ARE CRAZY! ANYWAY... THIS WILL ALL BLOW OVER SOON...

QUESTIONS

· What would you have said to Jesus if you saw Him outside the tomb? Would you thank Him? Would you worship?

· Pray these things to Him now.

WHAT NOW?

ALL AUTHORITY IN HEAVEN AND ON EARTH HAS BEEN GIVEN TO ME...

THEREFORE

J

GO!

SAME MESSAGE TO DOUBTERS... 28:17

...AND THE FAITHFUL!

This might be the end of our walk through Matthew together, but this isn't the end of *your* journey – it's only the beginning!

FULL AUTHORITY OF THE KING (28:16-18)

Whether it's Caesar or the U.S. President, the most powerful person on earth is not a scratch on the authority of King Jesus. When Jesus meets His disciples after rising from the dead, He tells them something has changed – He has been given ultimate authority over heaven and earth.

This means there has been fanfare and a royal coronation in heaven! The Father has crowned the Son of God as King. The Son of Man will rule forever (check out Daniel 7:13–14). Jesus has been made King over absolutely everything! So ... what happens now?

THE KING'S COMMAND (28:19)

So you've become a Christian and are in God's Kingdom, guess that's the end of the story right? No way! The Christian life is exciting and the King's command gives your existence meaning, purpose and responsibilities.

Christians get to know Jesus personally. You can pray to Him, and hear Him speak to you through the Bible. If you don't know how best to do this – ask a Christian you know for help! Jesus also commands His disciples to 'Go!' – to enter into the world trusting in His power, helping others follow Jesus just as we have done. Amazingly, all our work, both in loving action and Kingdom message spreading, has everlasting significance. In fact, one day *you will meet* all the people you helped enter God's Kingdom from around the world (Revelation 7:9). This is a life worth living!

IMMANUEL – GOD WITH US (28:20)

Can you believe there were still people who doubted Jesus after seeing Him resurrected (v. 17)? Perhaps you too have some doubts about all this. It's hard being a Christian, and maybe you still have unanswered questions, so can you really trust Jesus?

The final words of Matthew's account are therefore not just for the disciples, but for you too. If you, like the disciples, have let Jesus down, these words are for you. If you, like the disciples, don't think you've got what it takes to follow Him, these words are for you. And if you, like the disciples, have no idea what scary and

MAT 28:20

exciting things await those who obey Jesus' command, these words are for you! The King of heaven and earth gives you a promise today: 'I am with you *always*, to the very end of the age.'

QUESTIONS

What happens next? You can see how the disciples responded to Jesus' instructions in the New Testament book of Acts. But what about you – how will you respond to Jesus' call?

WRITE NOTES HERE ...

WRITE NOTES HERE ...

10 Publishing

a division of **10** of those.com

10Publishing is the publishing house of **10ofThose**.
It is committed to producing quality Christian resources
that are biblical and accessible.

www.10ofthose.com is our online retail arm selling
thousands of quality books at discounted prices.

For information contact: **info@10ofthose.com**
or check out our website: **www.10ofthose.com**